PROPHECY

A GIFT FOR TODAY?

Foreword by
I. Howard Marshall

Graham Houston

INTERVARSITY PRESS
DOWNERS GROVE, ILLINOIS 60515

©*1989 by Graham Houston*

Published in the United States of America by InterVarsity Press, Downers Grove, Illinois, with permission from Universities and Colleges Christian Fellowship, Leicester, England.

InterVarsity Press is the book-publishing division of InterVarsity Christian Fellowship, a student movement active on campus at hundreds of universities, colleges and schools of nursing. For information about local and regional activities, write Public Relations Dept., InterVarsity Christian Fellowship, 6400 Schroeder Rd., P.O. Box 7895, Madison, WI 53707-7895.

Distributed in Canada through InterVarsity Press, 860 Denison St., Unit 3, Markham, Ontario L3R 4H1, Canada.

All Scripture quotations, unless otherwise indicated, are from the Holy Bible, New International Version. Copyright © 1973, 1978, International Bible Society. Used by permission of Zondervan Bible Publishers.

Cover photograph: Robert Flesher

ISBN 0-8308-1267-9

Typeset in Great Britain by Parker Typesetting Service, Leicester
Set in Linotron Baskerville

Printed in the United States of America ∞

Library of Congress Cataloging-in-Publication Data
Houston, Graham, 1950-
    [Prophecy now]
    Prophecy: a gift for today? / by Graham Houston.
        p.   cm.
    Originally published under title: Prophecy now.
    ISBN 0-8308-1267-9
    1. Bible—Prophecies.   I. Title.
    BS647.2.H68   1989
    231.7'45—dc20   *89-2176*
                                                           CIP

15	14	13	12	11	10	9	8	7	6	5	4	3	2	1
99	98	97	96	95	94	93	92	91	90	89				

For Irene

Acknowledgments

This book is a by-product of almost ten years of study on the New Testament's teaching on the Holy Spirit. The groundwork was postgraduate study under Professor I. Howard Marshall, to whom I am greatly indebted for that period of supervision, and for his helpful comments about this work.

The idea for a book arose out of a paper given at a ministers' conference, and I am grateful for the encouragement given by three of my colleagues in the Church of Scotland, Rev. Sandy Tait, Rev. William Still, and Rev. Dr Sinclair B. Ferguson.

Word-processing of the manuscript was cheerfully done by Pat Cameron, with help in photocopying by Mike Frew.

Thanks are also due to friends at Letham St Mark's Church, for their encouragement.

My wife Irene and our children Rachel, Rhoda and Stephen have been very patient with a rookie author, and I record my thanks with affection.

Graham Houston

Foreword

There must be something about Aberdeen which attracts students of prophecy, for it was while he was doing his doctoral studies at Aberdeen that Joel B. Green's most helpful book *How to Read Prophecy* (Leicester: IVP, 1984) appeared; I was so taken with its brilliant opening pages that I quoted them verbatim in a Sunday morning sermon in a local church, and they obviously made a hit.

Now Graham Houston, who studied for his MTh. at Aberdeen, has turned his attention to the same broad topic. But whereas Joel was concerned mostly with understanding Old Testament prophecy, Graham is interested primarily in the existence and activity of prophets in the New Testament churches and at the present day.

There has been a good deal of attention given to the character of biblical prophecy in recent years, spurred no doubt by fresh outbursts of prophetic activity in the contemporary church and by the need to assess these in the light of Scripture. But much of the discussion that really gets down to the roots of the matter is hidden from the ordinary reader in technical monographs. It is the virtue of this book that its author is a New Testament scholar who is familiar with the main scholarly discussions of prophecy, but he also has the gift of writing simply and clearly about the matter and he does so with an enthusiasm that carries his readers along with him.

I do not think that I am giving away any secrets if I say that Mr Houston has found himself changing his mind on various aspects of the activity of the Holy Spirit in prophecy and other charismatic gifts as he has studied the New Testament over the years. That is exactly as it should be, for what is the point of reading the Bible if it does not change us? He is concerned to find the truth and to share it with his readers, but at the same time he recognizes the legitimacy of different opinions and writes in an eirenic and charitable spirit.

I believe that readers who are puzzled by the variety of opinions about prophecy current in the churches today will be greatly helped by this presentation of the New Testament teaching, and I pray that all who read it will have a better appreciation of the work of the Spirit in the early days of the church and in our own time.

> Do not put out the Spirit's fire;
> do not treat prophecies with contempt.
> Test everything.
> Hold on to the good.
> Avoid every kind of evil. (1 Thes. 5:19–22)

I. Howard Marshall
University of Aberdeen

1/Will the real prophet please stand up?

The room was charged with expectation as a group of church leaders gathered in a well-known Scottish conference centre. They had come to share with each other and to learn from speakers who were acknowledged as experts in their field of interest: *prophecy*. During the first session the leader shared his perspective: God speaks today. Just as he long ago communicated his will and guidance, his praise and admonition, through prophets like Jeremiah, so God is still speaking through them to his church and to the world. In a day of unprecedented problems at home and abroad, who could have disagreed with the speaker's viewpoint? Surely the prophetic word, if it is available today, is desperately needed to shed light on a dark world? And who could deny that the church needs a personal message from God to assure his people of his guidance or his rebuke?

But what is prophecy? And what do people expect in terms of the prophetic word? We often use words without clearly defining what we mean by them, assuming that our hearers share our perspective. As part of my research for this book I carried out a survey of evangelical church leaders

11

in Scotland. I invited over two hundred to complete a questionnaire.[1] Of the 120 replies received, ten per cent were from elders or students for the ministry, and ninety per cent were from ministers. Most belonged to the Church of Scotland, which is Presbyterian in structure and Reformed in doctrine. I wanted to determine what my colleagues understood by the terms 'prophet' and 'prophecy' in the contemporary church.

The results were illuminating. Fifty-one per cent of those who responded considered themselves to be prophets or to have a prophetic ministry in their own terms. It is interesting to note that about one half of both ministers and laity were unwilling to think of themselves in this way. (Eighty-three per cent of the returns, however, suggested that prophecy would be exercised through preaching, sixty-five per cent through Bible study or prayer groups, and forty-two per cent through house groups.) From this we can glean that, while many church leaders believe that the prophetic word is still given by God to his church, many are reluctant to claim that they exercise a prophetic gift. This may be a sign of humility, or of a fear of being associated with those who may have made extreme claims to be prophets in recent times.

Seventy-five per cent of the sample did not expect prophecy to come through ministers only,

[1]The questionnaire was completed by 108 ministers and twelve others. Full details of the questions and responses are printed in Appendix 1, see pp. 202–203.

On p. 26, at the end of this chapter, the questionnaire is reproduced for you to fill in before reading the rest of this book.

and seventy-four per cent did not think of prophecy as exclusively a male domain. Yet only thirty-eight per cent expected prophecy in elders' meetings, and only twenty per cent thought that the prophetic word would be spoken in the secular work of Christians. It seems that the place for prophecy, in the expectation of most, was in the regular ministry of God's word. Despite that, the majority of ministers who replied said that they expected lay people to be involved in prophecy. This may reflect a feeling that, while preachers are called to proclaim the word of God for today, there is room for a response from other believers, both male and female, through which prophetic insights might come.

Another interesting result was that only sixteen per cent felt that the gift of prophecy had been withdrawn by God. It appears that the traditional Reformed view, that prophecy in all its forms died out with the closing of the canon of Scripture, is now unacceptable to many. It may be that the writings of authors such as the late David Watson have influenced theological opinion in this area; sixty-five per cent of those who replied were aware of his teaching on the subject of prophecy.

The results of the survey indicate that there is considerable confusion about prophecy in today's church. The concept is an elusive one to define, and people can use 'prophecy' and its associated words in different ways. The late Tommy Cooper, English comedian *par excellence*, had a joke in his repertoire which illustrates this: 'A man walked into a bar and said "Ouch" – it was an *iron* bar!' Words don't always mean what they

13

seem to mean on first encounter: we have to examine the context in which they arise.

The history of the use of a word is as important as its derivation. In any given context, the meaning of a word depends as much upon the place and use of the word as upon its supposed etymology. Because of this, the words associated with prophecy in the New Testament need not always be used to describe the same phenomena. We cannot assume that in every passage where prophecy is referred to we are dealing with the same meaning of the word. To confuse matters further there are many different scenarios for what purports to be prophecy in today's church. Let us examine seven possible scenarios.

Seven scenarios

Over the years I have come into contact with many claims to prophecy in the modern church. The prophetic gift may be claimed by prophets, or for them by their admirers; prophecy may be perceived as the preserve of a few gifted leaders who display remarkable insights; on the other hand it may be thought of in more commonplace terms as the birthright of every believer – a privilege which may be enjoyed by many.

The first scenario is a celebration during 'X Bible Week', an annual gathering of charismatic Christians, many of whom are associated with the house church ('Restoration') movement. During the worship time, in which singing led by a praise band is interspersed with spontaneous prayer and occasional dancing, a girl in her early twenties comes forward and speaks to the leaders on the platform. They permit her to come to the microphone to share a message. She says that the Lord has shown her a picture, which she then describes and interprets. It means, she says, that God is really with them to confirm his blessing on their fellowships. She uses scriptural phrases and images, and the message comes over in the first person: God is speaking personally to his people – at least that is the impression. Is *that* prophecy today?

The second scenario is quite different. In this a large number of conservative evangelical Christians have come to hear an address by a respected preacher about what he feels the future may hold for the church in their land. He says that he senses that they are on the edge of a very significant time, whether it be revival, persecution or even the second coming of Christ. He encourages Christians to be faithful and prayerful in what he believes will be days of crucial importance. As this message comes through one who is noted for his commitment to the systematic exposition of Scripture and his remarkable spiritual insight, the congregation notes his words carefully, considering him to be a prophetic figure. But *is* his message typical of prophecy today?

The third scenario takes up the story mentioned at the beginning of this chapter. In that conference, led by a minister who is acknowledged by many as a prophet, mention was made of an international gathering in which he had been involved. The purpose of the meeting had been to bring together people with acknowledged prophetic ministries, from all over the world, to try to discern what God was saying to his church

15

and doing in the world at large. After days of fasting and praying, he said, they came to a consensus that God was really shaking the world and the church. Their conviction was that Christians should not pray for the disturbance to stop but for it to take its course. Only then would people be awakened to their spiritual plight. In speaking of how the prophets came to such conclusions he emphasized that the study of Old Testament prophets such as Jeremiah and Haggai was central to their discussion. Is *that* prophecy today?

The fourth scenario also involves a large gathering of evangelical Christians. The visiting speaker from America is a noted exponent of social action. He rebukes his hearers for their lack of involvement in political and social issues, calling them to get involved with the poor. He reminds them of the Old Testament prophetic themes of justice and peace. Many of his admirers regard him as a modern prophet with a word of God's judgment which speaks pointedly to today's church. Is *that* prophecy today?

In the fifth scenario an American charismatic leader holds large conventions to teach church leaders to be open to spiritual gifts and to expect God to speak to their situations in vivid ways, often by giving remarkable insights into pastoral problems by supernatural means. In one illustration he recalls an incident during a flight between cities in the United States. Turning to greet the man sitting next to him he becomes acutely aware that God is telling him about his neighbour's life-situation: the man is an adulterer. He feels led to share his insight with him in private. As a result of the confrontation the man is converted, having

16

become overwhelmed by his guilt. Is *that* pheno-menon an example of prophecy today?

In the sixth scenario the wife of a prominent British pastor writes to one of her husband's col-leagues about his church which they have recently visited. She shares her strong conviction that, des-pite the present difficulties and opposition to the gospel, there will be a great spiritual harvest in due course. As the years go by the message proves to be amazingly accurate in its insights concerning the real condition of the church and the renewal which God begins. Is *that* prophecy today?

Finally, the seventh scenario concerns a book from the pen of a professor of theology who is well known for his defence of the Reformed faith. He writes to assure his readers that prophecy as described in the Bible has passed away with the completion of the canon of Scripture, and that only exhortation and application remain of the prophetic dimension in the proclamation of the word of God. Is *that* what our response should be to claims to prophecy today?

Is it any wonder that there is so much confusion about this subject when so many varied claims are made by sincere Christian people?

A historical perspective

To encourage those of my readers who may have shared my confusion, there is some comfort in the fact that great theologians of the past have not been united in their understanding of the nature of prophecy in the church.

From time to time various claims have been made concerning prophetic gifts, and church

17

leaders have responded in different ways over the centuries. Some have discarded such claims as worthless, believing that prophecy was limited to the age during which the Scriptures were being written and collected. Others have conceded that some aspects of prophecy may continue to survive as part of the spiritual endowment of the risen Lord to his church.

In some cases noted theologians have acknowledged that in their estimation others have possessed a genuine gift of prophecy. They believed that contemporaries were being used by God to bring a timely message to the church. An example of this was the reaction of the North African theologian Tertullian to the movement which came to be known as Montanism. Montanus, who hailed from Asia Minor (a region noted for its enthusiastic forms of religion), was acclaimed as a prophet in the second century AD. He led a movement which attracted a number of followers and was characterized by ecstatic phenomena. Eusebius, the noted historian of that period of church history, tells us that Montanus would find himself suddenly possessed and in a state of frenzy, raving and uttering strange sounds. He believed himself to be a mouthpiece of the Holy Spirit and Tertullian was among those who were influenced by his claims.

The majority of church leaders at that time, however, condemned the movement as heretical, and Tertullian eventually broke with the Catholic communion. In one of his works he records a description of what took place in Christian worship throughout the Roman Empire in his day: 'We come together ... to approach God in prayer ... to read the divine scriptures ... We also have *exhortations, rebukes, divine censures*.'[1] The last part of this quotation probably indicates the place of Christian prophecy in the life of the early church.

In the Middle Ages, Thomas Aquinas, one of the most influential Catholic theologians, wrote: 'In every period there have always been some who have the spirit of prophecy, not to set forth new teaching of the faith, but to give direction to human activities.'[2]

There are three important points in Aquinas' teaching on prophecy which will help us in our present survey. First, he thought of prophecy as a spiritual gift, a special and divinely inspired way of knowing which is given to some person within the church for the benefit of others and for the personal growth of the prophet; each prophetic revelation is a new giving of the Holy Spirit and is therefore a new way of relating to God. Secondly, prophetic knowledge in itself is thought of as revealed by God and absolutely certain; however, prophets are sinners and cannot always sort out what is from God and what is from themselves, so prophecy is subject to discernment. Thirdly, prophecy is given to God's people, the church, in every age for their upbuilding and guidance in Christian living.

It is interesting that Aquinas thought of prophecy in the church, not as the revelation of new

[1]Quoted in F. F. Bruce, *The Spreading Flame* (Exeter: Paternoster Press, 1958), p. 197. See also D. Wright, 'Montanism: a movement of spiritual renewal?', *Theological Renewal* 22 (1982), pp. 19–29.

[2]Aquinas, *Summa Theologica* 2.2, p. 74, quoted by R. Faricy, 'Charism of prophecy in the writings of Thomas Aquinas', *Theological Renewal* 19 (1981), pp. 16–21.

truths about the nature and purposes of God, but as the revealing of God's guidance to his people in their specific situation. His quoted statement is clear and unequivocal.

By the time of the Reformation of the sixteenth century, however, theological opinion on prophecy was not quite so precise. John Calvin, who is regarded by many as the greatest of the Reformers, wrote:

> Those who preside over the government of the church ... are called ... apostles, then prophets, thirdly evangelists, fourthly pastors, and finally teachers [Eph. 4:11]. Of these only the last two have an ordinary office in the church; the Lord raised up the first three at the beginning of the Kingdom, and now and again revives them as the need of the times demands.[1]

This suggests that, as they apply the teaching of his word, pastors and teachers are the regular means by which God exercises his rule and direction of the church. Yet Calvin admits that God may occasionally adopt a different strategy by the reviving of more unusual ministries such as apostles, prophets and evangelists. As to when the need of the times might demand such an intervention, Calvin is silent. History has conferred on Calvin the prophetic accolade which he did not claim for himself, but it is possible that in this reference Calvin is thinking of his great contemporary Martin Luther as one eminent example of the prophet extraordinary.

[1]J. Calvin, *Institutes of the Christian Religion*, tr. F. L. Battles, ed. J. T. McNeill (Philadelphia: Westminster Press, 1960), vol. 2, p. 1056.

Yet we must ask what Calvin understood to have been the nature of prophecy in the church. In another place he says: 'Paul applies the name "prophets" not to all those who were interpreters of God's will, but to those who excelled in a particular revelation [Eph. 4:11]. This class either does not exist today or is less commonly seen.'[1] From this we can glean that Calvin had a broad concept of the nature of revelation. He did not limit revelation to the revealing of God's words to man by means of divine inspiration of human speakers and writers. Clearly the 'particular revelation' to which he refers did not extend to messages which were later recorded in Scripture. Calvin had no doubt that the canon was closed and that the biblical words were from God himself as ultimate author. But there could be a secondary type of revelation which revealed God's will for particular situations. Calvin elucidates this point:

> These three functions [apostles, prophets, evangelists] were not established in the church as permanent ones, but only for that time during which churches were to be erected where none existed before, or where they were to be carried over from Moses to Christ. Still, I do not deny that the Lord has sometimes at a later period raised up apostles, or at least evangelists in their place, as has happened in our own day. For there was need for such persons to lead the church back from the rebellion of Antichrist. Nonetheless, I call

[1] *Ibid.*, p. 1057.

this office 'extraordinary', because in duly
constituted churches it has no place.[1]

This may refer again to Luther and his like,
whose authority and influence can under God
change the course of human history. Calvin was
remarkably open to the possibility that God might
do a new thing which was out of the ordinary if
the situation demanded that. He was convinced
that the regular pattern of God's communication
to his people was through the systematic exposition of the Bible, a task which was his life's work
(weekdays as well as Sundays!). Yet he accepted
that at crucial points in the unfolding of God's
purposes prophets might be raised up if God so
willed.

Despite that, we are left with an impression that
Calvin was rather uncertain about the distinctions
between pastors, teachers, prophets and apostles:
'Next come pastors and teachers, whom the
church can never go without ... For as our
teachers correspond to the ancient prophets, so
do our pastors to the apostles ... But the office of
teachers is very similar in character [to that of
prophet] and has exactly the same purpose.'[2] In
the light of what Calvin says, is it any wonder that
we (of small brain by comparison with such theological giants) find it difficult to come to terms
with prophecy as a phenomenon in today's
church? Because of this problem some Reformed
scholars have retreated into a 'no-go area' where
they insist that prophecy was simply one aspect of
the revelation of the word of God which was later

[1]*Ibid.*, parenthesis mine.
[2]*Ibid.*, pp. 1057–1058, parenthesis mine.

recorded in Scripture. But we must ask whether this does justice to the New Testament evidence and whether such a position can encourage a thorough investigation of modern prophetic claims. The danger is that valid prophetic insights might be rejected as spurious without a proper hearing.

Recent developments

So far our discussion has introduced us to prophecy as a matter which is of widespread interest and concern in today's church, and which many Christians (albeit in different ways) expect to be operative. We have noted that there are several possible scenarios for prophecy in the church and that this range of understanding tends to confuse the issue. Since 1960 the charismatic movement has become a major force in the world-wide church, affecting all the major denominations, including the Roman Catholic Church. Authors such as the late David Watson have been writing in a stimulating way, often bringing new insights to texts which have long been a source of difficulty.

New Testament scholars have added in-depth studies on prophecy in the early church, with works by David Hill,[1] Wayne Grudem[2] and David

[1] D. Hill, *New Testament Prophecy* (London: Marshall, Morgan & Scott, 1979). Dr David Hill is Reader in Biblical Studies at the University of Sheffield, UK.

[2] W. Grudem, *The Gift of Prophecy in 1 Corinthians* (Washington, DC: University Press of America, 1982). The research on this subject by Dr Wayne Grudem, currently Associate Professor of Systematic Theology at Trinity Evangelical Divinity School, USA, has been seminal. His doctoral thesis, submitted to the University of Cambridge in 1978, formed the basis of his book. A semi-popular version

Aune[1] extending our understanding of Christian prophecy in the New Testament. Another influential writer has been Clifford Hill,[2] whose editorship of the periodical *Prophecy Today* has enabled the debate to be widened by providing a clearing-house for what purports to be prophecy in the life of the modern church. In this is an earnest desire to learn what God is saying to his people in our generation, and no-one could fault such a concern.

Yet that objective must be firmly rooted in Scripture if it is to be of lasting value to the church of Jesus Christ and an encouragement to the extension of his kingdom. It is for that reason that the greater part of this book will be concerned with what the New Testament has to say about prophecy. In particular we will be asking what the New Testament writers expected Christian prophecy to be like in the experience of the early church, and whether they thought that it was a phenomenon which would die out after their day.

Seven questions

Recent research enables us to isolate seven major questions which must be answered satisfactorily if we are to get to the heart of the matter:

of his work on prophecy is his more recent *The Gift of Prophecy in the New Testament and Today* (Eastbourne: Kingsway Publications, 1988).

[1] D. Aune, *Prophecy in Early Christianity and the Ancient Mediterranean World* (Grand Rapids: Wm B. Eerdmans, 1983). Dr David Aune is Professor of Religious Studies, St Xavier College, USA.

[2] C. Hill, *Towards the Dawn* (London: Fontana Books, 1980); *The Day Comes* (London: Fontana Books,. 1982); *Tell My People I Love Them* (London: Fontana Books, 1983); *A Prophetic People* (London: Fontana Books, 1986).

1. What authority is claimed for prophecy in the Old and New Testaments?
2. What is the connection between apostles and prophets in the New Testament?
3. In the New Testament, is Christian prophecy an aspect of preaching/teaching?
4. Why is New Testament prophecy called 'revelation'?
5. What is the form, content and function of Christian prophecy?
6. Who are eligible and able to prophesy in the church, according to the New Testament?
7. What does Paul mean by 'where there are prophecies, they will cease' (1 Cor. 13:8)?

We will deal with these questions in detail in chapters 2 to 9. At the end of each chapter you will find questions for individual thought or group discussion which I hope will enrich your grasp of this important subject. Please look up the Scripture references if they are not quoted in full; this will enable a fuller appreciation of the force of the argument. In chapter 10 we will seek to apply our findings to the seven scenarios (already described) of what purports to be prophecy today.

First, we must examine the claims made for prophecy in the Old and New Testaments before seeking to understand the place of Christian prophecy in the early church. But before you begin chapter 2 I suggest that you answer the survey questions overleaf for yourself. (The results are found in Appendix 1 on pp. 202–203.)

25

PROPHECY TODAY?

Please answer the following questions without further research, to indicate your *present* response.

1. **Do you consider yourself to be a prophet or to have a prophetic ministry?**

   YES   NO   DON'T KNOW

2. **In the life of your congregation, where would you expect prophecy to be exercised?**

(i)	Through preaching:	YES NO	DON'T KNOW
(ii)	In elders' meetings:	YES NO	DON'T KNOW
(iii)	In house groups:	YES NO	DON'T KNOW
(iv)	In Bible study/ prayer meetings:	YES NO	DON'T KNOW
(v)	In secular work of members:	YES NO	DON'T KNOW
(vi)	Nowhere:	YES NO	

3. **By whom would you expect prophecy to be exercised?**

(i)	By ministers only:	YES NO	DON'T KNOW
(ii)	By men only:	YES NO	DON'T KNOW

4. **Is New Testament prophecy the same phenomenon as Old Testament prophecy?**

   YES   NO   DON'T KNOW

5. **Is prophecy a spiritual gift which God no longer gives to his church?**

   YES   NO   DON'T KNOW

6. **Please indicate if you are aware of what the following have written about prophecy in recent years:**

(i)	Clifford Hill:	YES	NO
(ii)	Jim Wallis:	YES	NO
(iii)	John Wimber:	YES	NO
(iv)	David Watson:	YES	NO
(v)	Donald Macleod:	YES	NO
(vi)	David Hill:	YES	NO
(vii)	Wayne Grudem:	YES	NO

7. **What office do you hold?**

   Minister: Elder: Others:

2/Prophecy in the Old Testament

The phenomenon of prophecy is not easy to define. Nor is it always clear what authority is claimed for the prophets' words. By *authority* we do not mean the degree to which a person may be qualified to prophesy by reason of calling or experience. (We think of that use of the word when we say, 'He spoke with authority', because the person seemed to know what he was talking about and commanded our attention.) Here we are rather thinking of authority in terms of something invested in a person by another of higher rank or influence. For instance, an ambassador is appointed with the authority of his national government; he speaks with their authority and passes on their views on policy. On occasion he may speak instead as a private citizen and offer his personal opinions, and if so his words will be taken accordingly.

When we look at prophecy in the New Testament, in chapter 3, we shall be concerned to discover what authority was claimed by or for prophets in the early church. Did they claim or was it claimed that they spoke for God as his ambassadors? If so, to what extent did they have freedom to choose the words to say? Were they thought of as

possessing the same kind of authority in all cases?
And what did the early Christians do in response to
prophecies?

We must begin a step further back, however, by
looking at the authority claimed for prophecy in
the Old Testament. It is most likely that the early
church took its cues from prophetic traditions in
the Old Testament. Most of the first Christians
were Jews who found in Jesus the Messiah who
fulfilled the law and the prophets. They shared
their message with people who revered Moses and
Elijah, at least at a popular level. They had been
taught by rabbis who on the whole had no doubt
that God had spoken of old through the great
prophets, and they longed for the restoration of
the prophetic word which they recognized had
been absent since the time of Malachi (400 BC).[1]

Classical Old Testament prophecy

There have been various attempts to define the
etymology of the word 'prophet' (nābī') in the
Hebrew of the Old Testament.[2] There is, however,
widespread agreement among scholars that at the
very least a prophet (in the classical sense) claimed
to be or was thought to be a messenger from God
or another deity – a spokesman. We associate the
prophetic message with such introductions as
'Thus says the LORD', and we think of prophets as

---

[1]This does not exclude the probability that cultural influences
from the Graeco-Roman world may have influenced the forms of
prophetic speech in the early church, see D. Aune, *Prophecy in Early
Christianity and the Ancient Mediterranean World* (Grand Rapids: Wm
B. Eerdmans, 1983), p. 277.

[2]R. L. Harris (ed.), *Theological Wordbook of the Old Testament* (Chicago: Moody Press, 1980), vol. 1, pp. 544–545.

on the whole claiming to speak with a divine authority which extended to the actual words spoken and written. In Exodus 7:1–2 we read that Aaron was called to be Moses' spokesman ('your brother . . . will be your *prophet*') so that Pharaoh would hear God's word. This kind of prophecy is found throughout the Old Testament.

Moses was perhaps the first to define the phenomenon, although it can be traced much further back in the history of God's people. On the eve of the re-entry of the children of Israel into Canaan, after forty years in the desert, Moses warned them not to imitate the religious practices of those whom they would displace. Sorcery and divination were commonplace, and both were thought of as ways of manipulating the will of the particular deity who was worshipped. In contrast, the people of God were not to think that they could use religion to further their own purposes. Their God, the LORD (Yahweh or Jehovah – 'I AM WHO I AM', Ex. 3:14), was a God who communicated his will clearly by means of his prophets. In fact Moses thought of himself as the archetypal prophet, according to Deuteronomy 18:15: 'The LORD your God will raise up for you a *prophet* like me from among your own brothers. You must listen to him.'

That was ultimately fulfilled in the Messiah, as indicated in the New Testament (Jn. 1:21; Acts 3:21–22; 7:37).

Moses saw this as being worked out in a succession of prophets who would continue to bring God's message to his people. He believed that God was speaking through him when he said:

> I will raise up for them a *prophet* like you
> [Moses] from among their brothers; I will put
> my words in his mouth, and he will tell them
> everything I command him. If anyone does
> not listen to my words that the *prophet* speaks
> in my name, I myself will call him to account.
> (Dt. 18:18–19)

In other words Moses thought of the prophet as
bringing the *actual words* of God to the people, so
that to ignore the prophetic message was tantamount to ignoring God himself. Such a position
of authority could not be claimed lightly, however,
and the prophetic word was to be tested. In fact
severe penalties were threatened in order to pre-
vent people from claiming to be prophets without
having a genuine message to proclaim: 'But a
prophet who presumes to speak in my name anything I have not commanded him to say, or a
prophet who speaks in the name of other gods,
must be put to death' (Dt. 18:20). If someone
dared to prophesy in the name of the LORD, the
people were to use their discernment. If the word
came true, then they were to accept that the person
was a true prophet, and vice versa (Dt. 18:22).
Another test is found in Deuteronomy 13:1–3,
where the false prophet is seen as one who seduces
his hearers from their allegiance to the true God,
even though his predictions come true.

This understanding of prophetic authority is
also found in the story of Elijah (*c.* 875 BC). Early in
that account we find Elijah visiting a widow in
Zarephath (now in modern Lebanon). She was
suffering greatly due to the famine which God had
caused as a result of Elijah's prayers against the evil

king Ahab. Her son was dying, yet Elijah assured her that God would help them. Of course, a miracle was granted in the production of food and the raising of the boy. Interestingly the woman's response was: 'Now I know that you are a *man of God* and that the word of the LORD from your mouth is the truth' (1 Ki. 17:24). This was not principally because Elijah had been used to perform a miracle; it was because his words, which he had claimed to be from the LORD, had been fulfilled. Elijah was truly a 'man of God', God's spokesman.

Elijah acts as a bridge between the Mosaic tradition and the writings of the prophets which are recorded in the major and minor prophets. The major (such as Isaiah and Jeremiah) and the minor (such as Amos and Micah) were united in the conviction that they brought the word of the LORD to the people. That word was not limited to one aspect of the message, as can be illustrated from the prophecy of Micah, a contemporary of Isaiah who prophesied *c.* 750 BC.

From Micah we can glean the essential elements of *canonical* prophecy in the Old Testament (*i.e.* prophecy which has been included in the *canon* of Scripture under the name of the author). Such prophecy was primarily a *forth*telling of God's word which could include an element of the *fore*telling of events yet to happen:

In the last days
the mountain of the LORD's temple will be
    established
  as chief among the mountains;
it will be raised above the hills,
  and peoples will stream to it.

31

Many nations will come and say,
'Come, let us go up to the mountain of the LORD,
     to the house of the God of Jacob.
He will teach us his ways,
     so that we may walk in his paths.'
The law will go out from Zion,
     the word of the LORD from Jerusalem . . .
All the nations may walk
     in the name of their gods;
we will walk in the name of the LORD
     our God for ever and ever.

(Mi. 4:1–2, 5)

The future was not seen in isolation. God's people were to live in the light of eschatology – God's ultimate purposes. The prophets brought this awareness of being caught up in the historical process which God would bring to a glorious end.

The main thrust of the prophetic message did not dwell upon things to come, however, but concentrated on God's will for his people in their temporal situation. It was to offer direction, praise or blame:

Woe to those who plan iniquity,
     to those who plot evil on their beds!
At morning's light they carry it out
     because it is in their power to do it.
They covet fields and seize them,
     and houses, and take them.
They defraud a man of his home,
     a fellow-man of his inheritance.

Therefore, the LORD says:
'I am planning disaster against this people,
     from which you cannot save yourselves.

You will no longer walk proudly,
    for it will be a time of calamity . . .'
'Do not prophesy,' their prophets say.
    'Do not prophesy about these things;
    disgrace will not overtake us.'
Should it be said, O house of Jacob:
    'Is the Spirit of the LORD angry?
    Does he do such things?

'Do not my words do good
    to him whose ways are upright? . . .
If a liar and deceiver comes and says.
    'I will prophesy for you plenty of wine and beer,'
    he would be just the prophet for this people!
                        (Mi. 2:1–3, 6–7, 11)

Micah was aware of having a message for his own day, and not merely a forecast of future events, and he knew that counterfeit prophets would try to get a hearing. In his prophetic self-awareness he was confident that his words would do his hearers good, whereas those of the false prophets were like poison. Because of that Micah was unafraid to warn of impending disaster and to summon the people to repentance:

Shepherd your people with your staff,
    the flock of your inheritance . . .

'As in the days when you came out of Egypt,
    I will show them my wonders,' [says the
        LORD] . . .

Who is a God like you,
    who pardons sin and forgives the transgression
    of the remnant of his inheritance?

You do not stay angry for ever
    but delight to show mercy.
You will again have compassion on us;
    you will tread our sins underfoot
    and hurl all our iniquities into the depths of the
      sea.

                (Mi. 7:14a, 15, 18–19)

But this promise of forgiveness was to be enjoyed only by those who truly turned to the LORD and demonstrated true repentance: 'He has showed you, O man, what is good. And what does the LORD require of you? To act justly and to love mercy and to walk humbly with your God' (Mi. 6:8).

Above all, the prophetic message was to encourage God's people that the LORD's purposes would be consummated in the coming of the Messiah and his heralding of a new age during which the message would go out to the ends of the earth:

'But you, Bethlehem Ephrathah,
    though you are small among the clans of Judah,
out of you will come for me
    one who will be ruler over Israel,
whose origins are from of old,
    from ancient times.' . . .

He will stand and shepherd his flock
    in the strength of the LORD,
    in the majesty of the name of the LORD his God.
And they will live securely, for then his greatness
    will reach to the ends of the earth.
    And he will be their peace.

                (Mi. 5:2, 4–5a)

Micah, as an example of the prophet who claimed to communicate the actual words of God to his people, brought something old and something new to his hearers. Much of his message was a timely application of truths previously revealed to Moses in the Torah (the law of God recorded in Genesis to Deuteronomy). At least one section of his prophecy was paralleled by Isaiah, who spoke to the same generation as Micah (*cf.* Mi. 4:1–3 and Is. 2:1–4). And in his forecast that the Messiah would be born in Bethlehem we have something quite unique in the Old Testament. Yet, whether repeating old truths or receiving new insights, his conviction was that the LORD was speaking through him and that those who prophesied an alternative message were impostors.

Other prophetic phenomena in the Old Testament

While the phenomenon of prophecy in the Old Testament is most often characterized by this claim to absolute verbal authority, there are some occasions where a type of prophecy is described which seems to have been regarded differently, not so much as a revelation of God's secrets but as a powerful sign of his presence with his people at crucial times in the unfolding of God's purposes.

An example of this is found in Numbers 11:24–30, where, after seventy elders have been appointed by Moses to help govern the people, it is said that they all prophesied together. This was not necessarily thought of as a message or messages from God, but was nevertheless seen to be a clear sign that the Spirit of God was among them (Nu. 11:25). Yet Moses records that those who prophesied on that day did not do so again.

At that time two men who were listed among the

35

elders did not go out to the Tent of Meeting with the others and so were not at first involved in the experience. The Spirit of God also rested on them, however (Nu. 11:26), and they prophesied in the camp. Joshua, Moses' right-hand-man, tried to stop them, fearing that this was a threat to Moses' authority. Moses' reply displays his legendary humility: 'Are you jealous for my sake? I wish that all the LORD's people were prophets and that the LORD would put his Spirit on them!' (Nu. 11:29).

This longing that God's people might know the reality of his Spirit in their midst must be qualified by what we have already noted from Deuteronomy 18 concerning prophecy immediately prior to the invasion of Canaan. In that passage Moses seems to discourage what he had encouraged about forty years earlier, as quoted in Numbers 11:29. To warn people that speaking presumptuously in the name of the LORD would be punished by death (Dt. 18:20) would surely have curbed all prophetic activity if Moses was thinking of the same kind of prophecy in both instances.

Some might say that Moses later regretted his quoted largesse and may have limited prophecy because it was getting out of hand. It is more likely, however, that Numbers 11 and Deuteronomy 18 are referring to different types of prophecy; one to an experience of being inspired to speak the actual words of God to the people (Dt. 18); the other to an experience of coming under the influence of the Spirit in such a way that it was evident that God was in the midst, prompting unusual behaviour or giving words of encouragement or praise, *etc.*, the general significance which was noted rather than any detailed message (Nu. 11). What was important was that the latter would be a blessing to God's people in confirming his presence with them.

Another example of this secondary type of prophecy is probably found in the history of King Saul (c. 1000 BC). Samuel had anointed Saul as king, and he told him that he would meet a procession of prophets coming down from the holy place at Gibeah. Samuel promised that the Spirit of God would come upon Saul in power and that he would prophesy with them (1 Sa. 10:5–6). This was to be a sign that God was in their midst. It would change Saul into a different person. Samuel's forecast came true, and the change in Saul made such an impact that an ironic proverb was made up: 'Is Saul also among the prophets?' (1 Sa. 10:9–12).

But despite the fact that Saul prophesied with those who were accepted as prophets, no record has remained of what Saul actually said. It is unlikely that his prophecy brought some important message for God's people, and it did not seem to claim to do so. The phenomenon of speaking spontaneously or acting in an unusual manner under the influence of the Spirit does not appear to have been subject to the scrutiny advocated by Moses in Deuteronomy 18. The popular reaction to Saul's prophecy may have been sceptical, but it was not judged to be contrary to the Mosaic guidelines.

The secondary type is probably found again in 1 Samuel 19:20–24. There an incident from the time of the flight of David from Saul is recorded. David escaped to Samuel's base at Ramah, and when Saul learnt of his whereabouts he sent men to capture him: 'But when they saw a group of prophets prophesying, with Samuel standing there as their

37

leader, the Spirit of God came upon Saul's men and they also prophesied' (1 Sa. 19:20).

Eventually Saul himself went to Ramah, and the Spirit of God came upon him and he walked along prophesying (1 Sa. 19:23). Again, there is no record of what any of the prophets may have actually said (if indeed they said anything significant) while under the influence of the Spirit.

We can see, therefore, that there is considerable evidence in the Old Testament for at least two types of prophecy, one of which claimed to communicate God's word with an absolute verbal authority, and one which was seen as a powerful sign of God's presence without necessarily bringing a specific message. The distinction is probably further seen in the prophecy of Joel. A good case has been made for considering Joel to be among the earliest of the canonical prophets (*c.* 800 BC).

If this is so, Joel provides an important link between the age of Elijah and the later prophets. We have noted that in Elijah's day there was a popular expectation that God spoke through his prophets. The writer of 1 Kings also warns against ignoring such prophetic warnings as the one given by the prophet Micaiah ben Imlah to evil King Ahab, as recorded in 1 Kings 22:12–40. Before his death Ahab was warned by Micaiah: 'If you ever return safely, the LORD has not spoken through me' (1 Ki. 22:28). In the terms laid down by Moses in Deuteronomy 18 Micaiah was laying his life on the line! Yet he was not afraid to say, 'Therefore hear the word of the LORD' (1 Ki. 22:19). Like Elijah, his credibility was open to test (*cf.* 2 Chr. 18: 1–27).

Joel certainly considered himself to be a prophet with that kind of authority. His book is prefaced

38

'The word of the LORD that came to Joel' (Joel 1:1). Some scholars have suggested that Joel was quite influential in the formulation of the prophetic tradition, and it is possible that later prophets such as Amos, Micah, Zephaniah, Jeremiah and Ezekiel drew from Joel's prophecy, as there are striking literary parallels between their messages and his. It seems that they borrowed Joel's phrases in some instances.

In one quite distinctive passage Joel refers to a hope that prophecy would become an experience shared by many of God's people: 'And afterwards, I will pour out my Spirit on all people. Your sons and daughters will prophesy, your old men will dream dreams, and your young men will see visions. Even on my servants, both men and women, I will pour out my Spirit in those days' (Joel 2:28–29). This longing for the blessing of God's Spirit is seen again in Ezekiel 39 and in Zechariah 12 – 13 (see pp. 54–56). But nowhere else is it associated with an extension of the prophetic gift. The question is whether Joel's hope was akin to that of Moses ('I wish that all the LORD's people were prophets', Nu. 11:29) – or whether he looked for something else. We have suggested that Moses was not longing for all God's people to make claims to be authoritative spokesmen who would declare, 'Thus says the LORD'; he was keen to limit such prophecy and did not believe that all should attempt to prophesy in that way. But Moses longed for the manifestation of God's Spirit, and we have reasonable grounds for suggesting that Joel had a similar vision.

Of course, Joel's prophecy was to become a key part of Peter's preaching on the Day of Pentecost, but we will leave further comment on it until our next chapter (see pp. 53–58).

Prophecy in the Old Testament and Judaism

The main thrust of the prophetic tradition in the Old Testament is characterized by a claim to absolute verbal authority. This is exemplified by Moses, Elijah and the canonical prophets. A secondary type is also discernible, however, in which it was believed that the Spirit of God might move people to speak spontaneously and appropriately without inspiring the very words themselves. The result of such prophecy was to confirm God's presence with his people, but no detailed message was recorded and passed on.

After Malachi (c. 400 BC) the voice of authoritative prophecy was stilled. In the time between the Testaments many of the Jewish rabbis recognized that absolute verbal authority was a thing of the past. Many rabbis who accepted this cessation, however, also believed that prophetic phenomena were still operative in the inter-testamental period and in sub-apostolic times.[1]

This prophetic activity was expressed in predictions and extra-sensory perception, among other things. For example, one rabbi saw some women coming to visit him, and it is said that he saw by means of the Holy Spirit that one of them had just had a quarrel with her husband (see also pp. 189–191). Yet when rabbis expressed their insights they often linked them with previous revelations

[1]W. Grudem, *The Gift of Prophecy in 1 Corinthians* (Washington, DC: University Press of America, 1982), pp. 24–33.

recorded in Scripture. They said 'It is written' rather than 'Thus says the Lord'.

Of course any reference to rabbinic Judaism is of limited value in establishing the biblical view on prophecy, but it does confirm that our interpretation has a historical basis and is not a novelty.

The purpose of this chapter has not been to give an exhaustive account of prophecy in the Old Testament and Judaism, but to demonstrate that it is unneccesary to assume that the Hebrew/Aramaic terminology describing prophetic phenomena always refers to a claim to absolute verbal authority. In fact, there is much evidence for prophecy which made no such claim. While the phenomena associated with secondary prophetic activity may vary, we must now see if a similar distinction is discernible in the New Testament.

For further thought and discussion

1. What qualities and qualifications made Moses the supreme example of the classical Old Testament prophet?
2. In what ways was Jesus like Moses, in fulfilling Deuteronomy 18:15–19?
3. How would you react to somebody who made such claims for himself today?
4. What aspects of classical Old Testament prophecy are still available for church leaders today?
5. Read Joel 2:28–29. In what way does this point to the fulfilment of Moses' longing that all the Lord's people might be prophets?

3/Prophecy in the New Testament

We have established that references to prophets and prophecy in the Old Testament are not necessarily describing claims to absolute verbal authority. We have noted that along with the classical tradition of the prophets who said 'Thus says the LORD' there is evidence for prophetic activity which made no such claims, but which served as a powerful sign of the presence of God's Spirit at significant times. We must now enquire whether prophecy in the New Testament can be classified in a similar way.

John the Baptist was considered by Jesus to be the last of the prophets who prepared the way for the Messiah, in fulfilment of Malachi 3:1, which pointed to the coming of one like Elijah as a forerunner. Matthew quotes Jesus as saying of John:

> Then what did you go out to see? A prophet?
> Yes, I tell you, and more than a prophet ...
> For all the Prophets and the Law prophesied
> until John. And if you are willing to accept it,
> he is the Elijah who was to come. He who has
> ears, let him hear. (Mt. 11:9, 13–15)

In this way, Jesus emphasized the fact that God

42

had used his authoritative spokesmen over the centuries. Not only were those labelled 'prophets' in the Old Testament bearers of the words of God, but also all who were involved in the oral and written traditions which were gathered together to form the law and the prophets. When Jesus said that *all* the law and the prophets prophesied, he indicated that the fundamental nature of the Old Testament is prophetic. While scholars may try to classify different forms and styles of speech and writing (poetry, history, prophecy, *etc.*), this does not deny that there is one common factor: it is all God's prophetic word, and therefore absolutely authoritative.

Prophecy in the New Testament which claims an absolute verbal authority

Jesus' ministry

An example of this is found in Matthew 10:19–20, where Jesus is seen promising the twelve disciples before their first mission: 'At that time you will be given what to say, for it will not be you speaking, but *the Spirit of your Father speaking through you.*' The words 'prophet' or 'prophecy' are not used in these verses. At the end of the discourse, however, Jesus says: 'He who receives you receives me and he who receives me receives the one who sent me. Anyone who receives a *prophet* because he is a prophet will receive a *prophet's* reward . . .' (Mt. 10:40–41).

Although this may reflect a proverbial saying, it appears that Jesus applied the word 'prophet' both to himself and to his disciples. There is no doubt that Jesus spoke with the kind of absolute authority seen in the Old Testament tradition established by

Moses. In fact, 'Thus says the LORD' is often replaced by 'Truly, truly I say to you', in the sayings of Jesus. Our concern here, however, is to understand the authority of his messengers.

Jesus promised that God would give his spokesmen words to say: 'Do not worry about what to say or how to say it' (Mt. 10:19). The *form* ('how') and the *content* ('what') were to be given to them by the Spirit. This was associated with their bearing witness before councils, governors and kings, which Jesus predicted would be a feature of their ministry. In reality the details of this were more fully worked out in the early chapters of the book of Acts. There the apostles are seen defending the faith before the Jewish Council, the Sanhedrin, in Jerusalem (Acts 4:1–22; 5:17–42; 7:1–60), and Luke clearly presents them as authoritative spokesmen of God to his people.

The apostles in Acts 1 – 7

Later in this chapter we will look at the preaching of Peter at Pentecost and seek to understand the significance of prophecy in the new age which began then. At this stage, however, we want to follow up Jesus' prediction that the apostles would be given a message despite the opposition. Luke clearly portrays the apostles themselves as the true inheritors of the classical prophetic tradition. Acts 4:8 says that Peter was filled with the Holy Spirit when he addressed the rulers and elders in Jerusalem. What follows is a summary of a courageous speech in which Peter explains that the healing of the lame man at the gate of the temple (Acts 3:1–26) was the result of the present power of the risen Jesus. Peter's eloquence was clearly beyond his natural powers (Acts 4:13). He could not help speaking about what he had seen and heard (Acts 4:20). He spoke a message which he believed was from God himself, disobedience to which he could not consider (Acts 4:19). In addition, it was a message which was powerfully applied to the situation of the day. It rebuked the leaders of the Jews for crucifying Jesus (Acts 4:10) and claimed an authority far above that of the Sanhedrin. It would therefore have been seen by the people as a claim by the apostles to be at least as authoritative as the classical prophets of Old Testament times. In fact Peter spoke of Jesus as the supreme prophet in fulfilment of Moses' words (Dt. 18:15) in Acts 3:22–23, and emphasized that the Jews were heirs of the prophetic promises (Acts 3:25).

Again, after their release, the apostles were re-arrested and brought to trial. Once more they repeated the message in the power of the Holy Spirit (Acts 5:17–32). The reaction of the Jewish leaders was predictable: they wanted to put the apostles to death. Such claims were in their estimation tantamount to a contravention of what Moses had said about false prophets.

In fact, the advice of Gamaliel, which stopped their scheme, could be understood in terms of the same Mosaic provision. We noted that Moses in Deuteronomy 18:20 demanded that the false prophet was to be put to death if it was found that his message failed to come true. So Gamaliel, the wise rabbi at whose feet Saul of Tarsus sat, counselled his colleagues to take a similar course of action (Acts 5:34–39). If their message was from God nobody would be able to stop the apostles. If they were deluded they would suffer the same fate as

many other false claimants had done. The Sanhedrin had to wait and see.

Another example of the prophetic word which
clearly claimed to be God's words to man is seen in
the speech of Stephen before the Sanhedrin (Acts
7). This contains a survey of the Old Testament
history from Abraham to Solomon. It shows how
the official leaders of God's people consistently
persecuted the prophets (see Acts 7:51–53). By
being faithful to the prophetic tradition Stephen
had signed his own death warrant (*cf.* Jas. 5:10)!

As noted earlier, authoritative prophecy in the
biblical tradition did not always proclaim a new
revelation, but could be a timely application of
truth which had been revealed before. What is
significant about the apostles' message at this point
is the powerful and authoritative way in which they
made known what God had given them to say. The
self-awareness of the apostles (and of their associates like Stephen) seems to have been very similar
to that of the Old Testament prophets who, like
Jeremiah, felt that they had words from God to
share which they could not keep to themselves.

Whenever I speak, I cry out
   proclaiming violence and destruction.
So the word of the LORD has brought me
   insult and reproach all day long.
But if I say, 'I will not mention him
   or speak any more in his name,'
his word is in my heart like a fire,
   a fire shut up in my bones.
I am weary of holding it in;
   indeed, I cannot.

                       (Je. 20:8–9)

Compare that with the apostolic experience: 'We cannot help speaking about what we have seen and heard' (Acts 4:20) and 'We must obey God rather than men!' (Acts 5:29).

There is no doubt that Luke understood the ministry of the apostles as involving more than a renewal of the classical prophetic tradition. (In chapter 5 we shall think further about the teaching and preaching in which the apostles also engaged, and seek to understand what was distinctive about their prophetic ministry.) Luke's portrayal of the apostles places them on a par with their Old Testament forerunners, the canonical prophets, and shows that like them they were willing to suffer for the message which they proclaimed. In chapter 4 we shall look more closely at the apostles as prophets in the early church. Specifically, we shall examine Paul's references in Ephesians to 'the foundation of the apostles and prophets' and 'revealed by the Spirit to God's holy apostles and prophets' (Eph. 2:20; 3:5).

Revelation, 2 Peter and Jude

John's Revelation also claims an authority akin to classical Old Testament prophecy. The whole book is introduced by what purport to be words from the risen Christ through John to the churches, and the letters to the seven churches of Asia claim to be 'what the Spirit says to the churches' (Rev. 2:7, 11, 17, 29; 3:6, 13, 22). At its close Revelation includes this warning:

> I warn everyone who hears the words of the prophecy of this book: If anyone adds anything to them, God will add to him the plagues

described in this book. And if anyone takes words away from this book of prophecy, God will take away from him his share in the tree of life and in the holy city, which are described in this book. (Rev. 22:18–19)

This leaves us in no doubt that prophecy, as the communication of the actual words of God to his people, was understood by the New Testament writers to have been operative in their day.

In fact Peter recognized the need to distinguish this kind of authentic, authoritative prophecy from counterfeits or perhaps from less authoritative kinds of prophecy. He says: 'Above all, you must understand that no *prophecy of Scripture* came about by the prophet's own interpretation. For prophecy never had its origin in the will of man, but men spoke from God as they were carried along by the Holy Spirit' (2 Pet. 1:20–21).

Peter wanted to counteract the influence of false prophets in the churches (2 Pet. 2:1–3) who had even cast aspersions about the writings of Paul which were already in circulation: '[Paul's] letters contain some things that are hard to understand, which ignorant and unstable people distort, as they do *the other Scriptures*' (2 Pet. 3:16). At the very least, Peter placed Paul alongside the canonical prophets of the Old Testament and included his writings in his own canon of Scripture. In so doing, Peter may be placing Paul within the prophetic tradition and distinguishing him from false prophets. In fact Peter may well be claiming that for himself when he says in 2 Peter 1:19, 'We have the word of the prophets made more certain'.

This sense of the fulfilment of prophecy in New

Testament times is further seen in Jude 17–18, with reference to the prophetic words of the apostles: 'But, dear friends, remember what the apostles of our Lord Jesus Christ foretold. They said to you, "In the last times there will be scoffers who will follow their own ungodly desires."' This is expanded upon in 2 Peter 3:2–4, which scholars believe is dependent upon Jude. There Peter directly links the predictive message of Old Testament prophets with that of New Testament apostles: 'I want you to recall the words spoken in the past by the holy prophets and the command given by our Lord and Saviour through your apostles.

'First of all, you must understand that in the last days scoffers will come . . .'

Paul

The apostle Paul was aware of being involved in the prophetic word when he warned his friends in Thessalonica to be on their guard against counterfeit prophecy: 'we ask you, brothers, not to become easily unsettled or alarmed by some prophecy, report or letter supposed to have come from us, saying that the Day of the Lord has already come' (2 Thes. 2:1b–2).

Believers were to watch out for false prophecy and to test what they heard by comparing it with what they had already received from Paul: 'Don't let anyone deceive you in any way, for that day will not come until the rebellion occurs and the man of lawlessness is revealed, the man doomed to destruction' (2 Thes. 2:3). Paul's prophecy here bears all the hallmarks of the classical prophetic tradition as exemplified by Isaiah, Jeremiah and the other canonical prophets. He expected the churches to acknowledge his unique place in the flow of biblical history and theology, as one of the authors of the prophetic writings we call the New Testament.

Paul not only claimed to be an ambassador of Christ who communicated the very words of God (2 Cor. 5:20) and had the mind of Christ (1 Cor. 2:16). He is also portrayed in Acts, by Luke, as one who experienced dreams and visions. In Acts 18:9–10 (*cf.* Acts 23:11; 27:23–24), we read of such an experience which he had in Corinth after the initial preaching of the gospel had led to violent opposition from the Jewish community and immediate success among the Gentiles. In this stormy atmosphere Paul doubtless wondered whether his stay would be brief, as it had been in Thessalonica in Macedonia (Acts 17:1–9), and in Athens (Acts 17:16–34). Luke records that it was due to a vision at night that Paul stayed for a year and a half at Corinth, teaching the word of God: 'Do not be afraid; keep on speaking, do not be silent. For I am with you, and no-one is going to attack and harm you, because I have many people in this city' (Acts 18:9–10).

The phraseology of this prophetic word is very similar to messages of assurance which were received and communicated by the prophet Isaiah (Is. 41:10; 43:1–2, 5). Although Isaiah's words were directed to the people of God in exile, they doubtless spoke first of all to the prophet himself. He encouraged them to believe that God had not abandoned them: 'So do not fear, for I am with you . . . I will strengthen you and help you' (Is. 41:10). 'Do not be afraid' was part of Isaiah's message of comfort in which he was to speak tenderly to the people of Jerusalem (Is. 40:1) regarding the future return of God's people to their land after exile in Babylon.

No doubt Paul's experience of God's comforting word was shared with the newly founded congregation in Corinth, and established him in the classical prophetic tradition, a claim which clearly infuriated the Jews who remained unconverted.

Later, in similar vein, Paul was to write these words to the Corinthians: 'Praise be to the God and Father of our Lord Jesus Christ . . . who comforts us in all our troubles, so that we can comfort those in any trouble' (2 Cor. 1:3–4). It was Paul's awareness of being a bearer of the comforting word of God that encouraged him to accept his role as an authoritative spokesman of the God of all comfort.

Other prophetic phenomena in the New Testament

During my postgraduate studies I had no doubt that prophecy in the New Testament was (on the whole) to be understood as claiming an authority which extended to the actual words spoken and written. I understood the apostles to have been the true successors of the classical Old Testament prophets and believed that their message, collected in what we call the New Testament Scriptures, completed the revelation of the word of God. No doubt many prophetic words may not have been recorded, and there is evidence that some letters have been lost, but I was unwilling to think of prophecy in New Testament times as anything other than a phenomenon which was required in order to complete the canon of Scripture, or at least to provide the church with authoritative guidance until Scripture was complete. I would have conceded that the prophetic tradition in the New Testament did include an element of what David Hill[1] calls 'pastoral preaching', in which the prophet brought 'strengthening, encouragement and comfort' (1 Cor. 14:3) to the assembled church.

But this conclusion raised several questions. If prophecy was always associated with the reception and application of verbal revelation, an activity particularly associated with the apostles, why were women, who could prophesy (1 Cor. 11:4–5), excluded by Paul from exercising a teaching authority in the churches (1 Tim. 2:12), and why were none included among the definitive group of apostles? And if prophecy was always akin to that of the Old Testament canonical prophets, why did Paul encourage all Christians to seek the gift (1 Cor. 14:1)? In view of the Mosaic tradition which discouraged people from 'having a go' at prophecy, is it likely that Paul, with his rabbinic background, would want to open the floodgates of false prophecy? Finally, if Paul's concept of prophecy was that it was a communication of the very words of God to his people, why did he say 'we prophesy in part' (1 Cor. 13:9)?

It was with a sense of relief that I found a way through this thorny maze! Wayne Grudem[2] notes that a number of scholars have suggested that (as in the Old Testament) there are two prophetic strands in the New Testament. The primary type is indeed a continuation of the great tradition which

[1]D. Hill, *New Testament Prophecy* (London: Marshall, Morgan & Scott, 1979), p. 126.
[2]W. Grudem, *The Gift of Prophecy in 1 Corinthians* (Washington, DC: University Press of America, 1982), pp. 54–113.

proclaimed the words of the LORD. The secondary type, like the sign-gift which we noted in the experience of Moses' elders and King Saul, made no claims to bring any absolutely authoritative message to God's people. In what follows, we will call this 'New Testament prophecy' or 'Christian prophecy'.

Pentecost

That powerful signs of God's presence (in which it was impossible to say that a particular message was being communicated) could be designated as prophecy is seen in Acts 2. On the Day of Pentecost 120 believers were gathered together, and when the Holy Spirit came upon them they spoke out spontaneously about the wonders of God in words of languages which were previously unknown to the speakers. Observers overheard them, but there is no record of what they actually said, other than that they were 'declaring the wonders of God' (Acts 2:11). Like those who observed on that day, we might well ask: 'What does this mean?' (Acts 2:12).

Peter's address to that astonished crowd is presented by Luke as an explanation of the phenomena of Pentecost. As Joel had promised:

In the last days, God says,
I will pour out my Spirit on all people.
Your sons and daughters will prophesy,
your young men will see visions,
your old men will dream dreams.
Even on my servants, both men and women,
I will pour out my Spirit in those days,
and they will prophesy.

(Acts 2:17–18 quoting Joel 2:28–29)

53

Clearly, Peter's concern was not merely to explain what had happened on that day. The future tense in Greek can point to continuous action in the future; something which will begin at a particular point in time and continue. Peter is confirming that 'the last days' predicted by Joel have arrived, and that the phenomena observed on the Day of Pentecost are signs of a new age in which the Holy Spirit will be poured out as never before. Prophecy was seen as an important aspect of this outpouring, and Peter is quoted as using words which are not found in Joel's original, when in Acts 2:18b he says: '. . . and they will *prophesy*'. Prophecy, by both men and women, is to be a feature of spiritual experience 'in those days' – the last days between the Day of Pentecost and the Day of Judgment.

The idea of an outpouring of the Spirit is also found in Ezekiel 39:25–29, where the prophet, addressing the exiled Jews in Babylon, promises his people that the sovereign LORD has a message of hope for them. They will be brought back from captivity to their homeland, restored as a nation, and renewed in their faith: 'I will no longer hide my face from them, for I will pour out my Spirit on the house of Israel, declares the Sovereign LORD' (Ezk. 39:29).

Again, in Zechariah, who prophesied to the returning exiles, there is a promise of an outpouring of the Spirit:

> And I will pour out on the house of David and the inhabitants of Jerusalem a spirit of grace and supplication. They will look on me, the one they have pierced, and they will mourn . . . On that day a fountain will be opened to the

house of David and the inhabitants of Jerusalem, to cleanse them from sin and impurity.
(Zc. 12:10; 13:1)

In Joel, Ezekiel and Zechariah, the Hebrew word
shaphak is used for 'outpouring'. This word is
associated in the Old Testament with the pouring
out of blood or water in sacrifices and offerings,
symbolizing atonement and purification. God's
wrath is also described as being 'poured out' in the
Old Testament, as is man's anguish and complaint
in prayer. However the concept of outpouring
may be viewed, one thing is clear. It describes
phenomena which are either visible or audible to
the participants and observers. Whether it be in
the rites of sacrificial worship, in prayer, or in the
mighty acts of God's judgment, the pouring out is
seen or heard. When the reference is to the outpouring of the Spirit, therefore, events of great
significance are being described.

In Joel the visible signs would be the extension of
the prophetic gift to male and female, young and
old, so that many others would seek salvation. For
Joel this would be the revolutionary hallmark of a
new age when the Spirit's work would not be
restricted to the people of Israel, nor limited to
certain persons who were chosen for specific functions, such as prophets, priests or kings. Moses'
longing that *all* the LORD's people might be prophets would be realized. In a similar way Zechariah
looked for a new spirit of prayer and repentance
among God's people which would lead them into
an overwhelming experience of forgiveness and
cleansing from sin. Ezekiel expected God to vin-
dicate his holiness visibly, and looked for an end to

the times of judgment during which God had withdrawn the blessing of his Spirit, so that other nations would see that the LORD was in their midst.

On the Day of Pentecost Peter realized that the hopes of the prophets had indeed been fulfilled. The outpouring of the Spirit had begun. That day many in Jerusalem mourned for their sin of crucifying the Messiah. Many found a fountain of cleansing from sin and a new life in Christ. Many began to share the burden for prayer which had been the preliminary to that outpouring of the Spirit (Acts 1:14). God was no longer hiding his face from them: his presence was out in the open! The sign was that the struggling group of disciples (male and female) who had met in fear and trembling for fifty days since the first Easter were given the remarkable ability to declare the wonders of God in languages which they had never learnt, as the Spirit enabled them to speak.

The interesting thing is that Peter did not focus upon the speaking of strange tongues, as he might have done. He could have quoted from Isaiah, as Paul later did, and referred to tongues as a mighty sign of God's judgment:

In the Law it is written:
'Through men of strange tongues
and through the lips of foreigners
I will speak to this people,
but even then they will not listen to me'.
(1 Cor. 14:21, quoting Is. 28:11–12)

Instead, in response to the question: 'What does this mean?' (Acts 2:12), Peter does not focus upon the speaking of strange tongues at all, other than to say that the phenomenon is a clear sign that Jesus has been exalted to the right hand of God the Father and that the promised Holy Spirit has been poured out as Jesus had predicted (Acts 2:33, *cf.* 1:5).

What is more important to Peter, and to Luke, the historian who records the outline of his address, is that the church of Jesus the risen Lord is to be a *prophetic* church. *'They will prophesy'* (Acts 2:18) is assured by the remarkable scene of 120 men and women praising God in unknown languages. While, as we shall see, speaking in tongues continued to be valued by the early Christians, it was never compared to the prophetic gift in terms of importance for the upbuilding of the church.

It is not clear whether Peter thought of the Pentecostal tongues phenomenon as part of the prophetic experience itself or whether it was seen as the prelude to a new age of prophetic activity. It does not seem to matter. What is significant for our discussion is that prophecy, in the sense predicted by Joel, began to be experienced as part of the outpouring of the Spirit which heralded the last period of human history. As in the Old Testament record (as we have already noted), prophecy may take the form of inspired speech which makes no claims to be a communication of the very words of God, and which involves speaking under the influence of the Spirit in some non-specified way which confirms the presence of God and his attitude towards his people. The words spoken are never recorded, but the impression made by the phenomenon is, and an explanation is included in the account. So at Pentecost. We have no record of what may have been said in terms of spontaneous prophecy, but we do have an explanation of the

57

significance of a type of prophetic speech which was to become a hallmark of the early Christian experience. It would be a means of convincing people of God's presence with his people, as Joel had hoped.

Some scholars have rightly pointed out that Pentecost was a unique occasion, and that the phenomena observed on that day were quite remarkable in their intensity and effect. The 'birthday' of the New Testament church was being celebrated, and birthday gifts were granted in abundance. That cannot be denied. But it is one thing to argue that the prophecy and tongues on that day were extraordinary examples of the exercise of those spiritual gifts; it is quite another matter to suggest that the phenomena *per se* were intended only for the 'launch event' of the Christian church. That prophecy continued to be of value to the early Christians and was considered to be part of the regular manifestation of the Spirit in the churches is clearly seen in Paul's letters. There is evidence, for example, that twenty years after Pentecost, prophecy of a secondary type was being exercised in Thessalonica, although very little is said about the phenomenon.

Thessalonica

Earlier we noted that Paul, like Peter, claimed a prophetic authority akin to Joel and the other canonical prophets who declared 'Thus says the LORD'. 'Am I not an apostle?' (1 Cor. 9:1) was his rejoinder to those who challenged his authority. Yet in Paul's letters we find evidence of another type of prophetic activity which was not necessarily exercised by the apostles and their associates and which Paul considered to be valid in its own way: 'Do not put out the Spirit's fire; do not treat *prophecies* with contempt. Test everything. Hold on to the good. Avoid every kind of evil' (1 Thes. 5:19–22). This suggests a form of prophetic speech which was granted to believers as they met together. While Paul encouraged discernment about what purported to be apostolic prophecy (as we have noted with reference to 2 Thes. 2:1–5, pp. 49–50), he would never have instructed the churches to sift his authentic messages for what was profitable and what was not. Yet here the same Thessalonian church is encouraged to 'Hold on to the good. Avoid every kind of evil' (1 Thes. 5:21–22). No doubt this means that they were to accept what was in conformity with the apostolic teaching, which declared the principles of God's will and was therefore 'good, pleasing and perfect' (Rom. 12:2), and to reject all that contradicted the revealed word of God.

David Aune focuses on the five imperatives which Paul uses in this short passage: 'Do not quench . . . do not despise . . . test . . . hold fast . . . abstain from'.[1] This means that Christians should not pour cold water on the manifestation of the Spirit through prophecy in the church. There were apparently some within that congregation who were resisting the impulses of the Spirit in this way. The testing was to be undertaken by the whole congregation, not by some restricted group, and was to be carried out in a rational way which did not depend upon special spiritual insight. In

[1] D. Aune, *Prophecy in Early Christianity and the Ancient Mediterranean World* (Grand Rapids: Wm B. Eerdmans, 1983), pp. 219f. (RSV).

other words a discussion would take place in which the prophetic word would be evaluated and compared with received apostolic teaching and practice. Of course, some prophecies might not be couched in a way that invited discussion. They might be words of encouragement or rebuke which met with acceptance or rejection without debate. Silence might be the result of such a reception, with the testing being carried out inwardly and spiritually.

Paul's mission to Europe, which had resulted in the establishing of the Thessalonian church, had been launched from Antioch in Syria. He is listed in Acts 13:1 as one of the prophets and teachers in the church, prior to his missionary travels. In fact his call to specific service as an itinerant church-planter resulted from a prophetic word which came during a time of worship and fasting (Acts 13:2). Prophecy associated with the setting apart of church workers is also noted of Timothy in 1 Timothy 1:18, 4:14. As Paul had experienced prophetic direction already in his ministry, it is likely that he encouraged the Thessalonians, a few years later, to be open to the same kind of guidance and encouragement.

Luke and Paul

In Acts 21 Luke describes a situation where prophecy seems to be similar in authority to that mentioned in 1 Thessalonians 5. Paul, with Luke, was on this way to Jerusalem at the end of his third missionary journey. He had told the Ephesian church leaders: 'I only know that in every city the Holy Spirit warns me that prison and hardships are facing me' (Acts 20:23). Yet Paul and Luke pressed on towards Jerusalem by sea. They landed at Tyre and went to stay with believers who, 'through the Spirit', urged Paul not to go on to Jerusalem (Acts 21:4). But, having evaluated what they said, Paul and Luke continued their journey, via the coastal sea-route to Caesarea. Clearly, if they had understood prophecy as an always absolutely authoritative message from God they would not have disobeyed their urgent warning, as there is no hint in the narrative that Paul and Luke considered the believers to have been false prophets.

Not long afterwards, Paul was staying in Caesarea with the evangelist Philip, whose four daughters prophesied (Acts 21:9). At that time a prophet called Agabus came down to the coastal city from Judea with a message for Paul: 'The Holy Spirit says, "In this way the Jews of Jerusalem will bind the owner of this belt and will hand him over to the Gentiles"' (Acts 21:11). He then acted out in dramatic fashion what he predicted. As a result Luke urged Paul not to go to Jerusalem. After discussion, however, they agreed with Paul that it was indeed God's will for him to proceed (Acts 21:14). If Agabus' prophecy had been thought of as an absolute verbal revelation from God by the Holy Spirit, or as a false prophecy discerned in terms of the Mosaic guidelines of Deuteronomy 18, it is most unlikely that Luke would have reacted as he did.

David Aune notes that this oracle has little relationship to Old Testament prophetic speech forms, despite the similarities of introduction. Classical Old Testament prophecy nearly always

61

provides a reason for the warnings conveyed in terms of an accusation. Here Paul's fate was not seen as a divine threat of punishment. Aune concludes that Luke has not modelled Agabus' oracle after classical Old Testament prophecy, but that it is derived from Christian tradition as received by Luke.[1] While Wayne Grudem agrees that this passage is one of the more difficult to classify in terms of the prophetic authority claimed, he notes that Luke's common practice of making prophetic fulfilment explicit where it occurs is not followed (*cf.* Lk. 4:21; 24:44; Acts 1:16; 3:18; 11:28; 13:27). The two predictive elements, concerning the binding and handing over of Paul, are clearly falsified by the subsequent narrative.[2]

Any prophetic message of this type, which purported to bring God's guidance (even to the apostle Paul), was to be weighed and discussed. In fact, if we insist that all prophecy was of the primary type, then Agabus would surely have been rejected as a false prophet, as neither of his predictions came true. Paul was *not* bound by the Jews but by the Romans, and the Jews did *not* plan to hand over Paul to the Romans but to assassinate him (Acts 21:27–35).

In other words, Luke, the great historian of the New Testament, is quite prepared to present an account of prophetic activity in which the message of prophets is subject to scrutiny and may contain elements which are not absolutely accurate. Yet at the same time the general content of the prophecy is portrayed as the result of the Spirit's influence and in the end God's will is seen to be done. It may

[1] *Ibid.*, p. 264.
[2] *cf.* Grudem, *Gift of Prophecy in 1 Corinthians*, pp. 79–82.

even be possible that Agabus' introductory formula made greater claims to authority than were warranted. Of course the most detailed description of the secondary type of prophecy in the New Testament is found in 1 Corinthians, to which we must turn.

Prophetic authority in 1 Corinthians

Paul wrote 1 Corinthians in about AD 55, towards the end of his three-year ministry in the city of Ephesus in Asia Minor. We must understand his teaching on prophecy in that letter not merely in terms of the situation in Corinth, which can be gleaned from 1 Corinthians, especially from chapters 12 to 14; it is also significant that Paul should have written about this subject from Ephesus at that particular time in his ministry.

Acts 19:1–12 contains details of an incident which happened at Ephesus during that period in Paul's life. It is the record of an encounter between Paul and twelve disciples of John the Baptist. They were unaware of the reality of the Holy Spirit (Acts 19:2), and after further instruction they were baptized into the name of the Lord Jesus. Paul placed his hands on them so that they spoke in tongues and prophesied. But the content of their prophecy was not noted by Luke. It was like the phenomenon observed on the Day of Pentecost (Acts 2:4,11) and at Caesarea (Acts 10:46), when believers spontaneously praised God in languages hitherto unknown by them and bore witness to the reality of God in their midst. The prophetic element constituted a sign of God's presence rather than revealing a secret about divine realities.

63

Paul's ministry in Ephesus was marked by unusual evidences of God's Spirit at work. His preaching and teaching in a public hall led to the evangelization of the entire province of Asia (modern Western Turkey), according to Acts 19:10. God performed extraordinary miracles through Paul (Acts 19:11–12) and he was also involved in a notable case of exorcism (Acts 19:13–16). This led to many renouncing pagan religion for faith in Jesus (Acts 19:17–20). After this, Paul made plans to go back to Corinth (Acts 19:21), and it was probably at this time that he wrote 1 Corinthians to prepare the way for his visit. His departure from Ephesus was precipitated by a riot (Acts 19:23–41)!

Paul's return to Corinth was intended to help the Christians there to deal with many problems which had arisen since his departure three years earlier. At that time Corinth was in many ways the chief city of Greece, with a population of 250,000 free people and about 400,000 slaves. It was a centre of Greek religion, with at least twelve temples, including the famous shrine of Aphrodite, the goddess of love, where temple prostitution was practised. Licentious behaviour was commonplace, as in many large seaports. Many of the problems in the church seemed to stem from that source of temptation.

1 Corinthians does not deal merely with immorality and other problems associated with pagan religion and lifestyle. The church had experienced a violent birth as a result of Paul's preaching. The original believers were converts from Judaism who were forced to leave the synagogue (Acts 18:1–17). They began to meet in a house nearby, and former synagogue officials

were prominent in church leadership. One can imagine the tensions between them and those who remained loyal to Judaism, despite the fact that the Christians had not chosen to separate from their Jewish brethren but had been forced to do so.

After Paul's time there, Apollos, an eloquent preacher, came to Corinth from Ephesus and many of the Corinthians were attracted to him as a leader. The result was that parties developed in the church, with some favouring Paul and others Apollos (1 Cor. 1:12). Worship had also become the focus of an unhealthy spirit of competition between believers. Matters were getting out of hand, and Paul had to write to enable them to worship in a more controlled manner without inhibiting the work of the Spirit in their fellowship.

The believers were competing over the gifts of the Spirit which had been received. Spiritual pride had made some feel superior to others, and the gift of tongues seems to have been elevated in their estimation out of all proportion to its real importance for the upbuilding of the body of Christ.

Because of this Paul encouraged them 'eagerly [to] desire the greater gifts' (1 Cor. 12:31) and to stop competing over the various workings of the Spirit such as tongues, prophecy, healing and teaching. They needed each other and had to worship and work together harmoniously. Yet this was not intended to discourage the exercise of spiritual gifts: 'eagerly desire spiritual gifts, especially the gift of *prophecy*' (1 Cor. 14:1). Here we have the clearest statement on prophecy in the New Testament church. Let us examine in detail what Paul says about it.

To begin with, Paul says that 'everyone who

prophesies speaks to men for their strengthening, encouragement and comfort' (1 Cor. 14:3). He contrasts this with the gift of tongues, which is a gift to be used chiefly for personal edification (1 Cor. 14:4a) rather than for the benefit of the assembled believers in worship. So Paul continues: 'he who *prophesies* edifies the church' (14:4b) and 'He who *prophesies* is greater than one who speaks in tongues' (14:5b). This might be thought of as strange. Paul is trying to counteract their tendency to overemphasize the gift of tongues, but in arguing against that imbalance he does not suggest that all gifts are equally important for the upbuilding of the church. He lists 'revelation or knowledge or prophecy or word of instruction' (14:6b) – 'intelligible words' (14:9) – as being of supreme importance. (We shall look at the meaning of these concepts in chapters 5 and 6.)

Whatever prophecy may have been like in Corinth, it was 'intelligible'. Paul reaffirms in 1 Corinthians 14:19: 'in the church I would rather speak five intelligible words to instruct others than ten thousand words in a tongue'. Prophecy was 'for believers' (1 Cor. 14:22) in that the appropriate context for the utterance of prophecy was in the assembly for prayer, worship and teaching. Yet it was also a powerful means of reaching any unbelievers who had been invited to join the worship service; it made a deep impression, bringing many to be convicted of their sin and to acknowledge that God was in their midst (1 Cor. 14:24–25).

Prophecy was a gift for which any believer might ask God (1 Cor. 12:31; 14:1), and it was to be exercised in the worship meeting along with hymns, instruction, tongues and interpretation (1 Cor. 14:26). Although it was possible that any believer might be granted a prophetic insight which he or she might share with the church, only two or three prophets were permitted by Paul to speak at any one service. This was a means of controlling a situation in which many more wanted to contribute at any one time, with ensuing chaos. It was not a rule of Paul that every service should include two or three prophetic utterances. Paul's guidance is *concession* rather than command, when he says: 'Two or three *prophets* should speak' (1 Cor. 14:29). In addition, this does not necessarily imply that there were accredited prophets in the church who alone were allowed to participate in the sharing of prophecy. It is possible that the title 'prophet' was applied by Paul to anyone who prophesied at any time, and that 1 Corinthians 14:26–33 indicates that everybody who wanted to be involved in prophecy could do so within the Pauline guidelines (see pp.132–147).

The main point is this: Paul's encouragement, 'Be eager to prophesy' (1 Cor. 14:39), would never have been given if Paul had understood prophecy only in terms of absolute verbal authority. The prophet who communicated the very words of God to the church was not able to hold back the message, as we have seen from the examples of Jeremiah and the apostles in Acts. Such prophets demanded to be heard, and their message could be received or they could be rejected as impostors. In the Corinthian church, however, as in Thessalonica (1 Thes. 5:19–21), prophecy was to be evaluated: 'the others should *weigh carefully* what is said' (1 Cor. 14:29). It is probable that 'the others' here

67

refers to the rest of the assembled worshippers, and not merely 'the other prophets'.[1] As in 1 Thessalonians 5:19–20, this form of prophecy was not considered to be a message which brought the very words of God to the people. It was rather a timely word of instruction, encouragement or rebuke which brought the general thrust of God's guidance to the church in each particular situation; that guidance was discerned only after the prophecy was weighed and discussed in the presence of the whole church.

This is quite different from the prophetic self-awareness of Paul as an apostle, who claimed to be absolutely authoritative in his statements to the churches. In 1 Corinthians 14:36–38 he challenges those who claim to be spiritually gifted and to have insights into what God is saying:

> Did the word of God originate with you? Or are you the only people it has reached? If anybody thinks he is a *prophet* or spiritually gifted, let him acknowledge that what I am writing to you is the Lord's command. If he ignores this, he himself will be ignored.

Here Paul expresses his sense of vocation as an apostle of Jesus Christ. We shall look more closely at his understanding of the relationship between apostles and prophets in our next chapter.

Prophecy in Corinth

Before we conclude this chapter, however, let us recall the significance of Paul's teaching on

[1]Grudem, *Gift of Prophecy in 1 Corinthians*, pp. 60–62; *cf.* Aune, *Prophecy in Early Christianity*, p. 219.

prophecy in 1 Corinthians. He wrote these words during his extraordinary Ephesian ministry. He had witnessed the power of the Holy Spirit in his dealings with those twelve disciples of John the Baptist who had prophesied when he prayed with them. Over in Corinth the Spirit was also at work in the church, but there was a danger of misplaced zeal. Paul wanted them to find a balance in their experience. Far from discouraging their interest in spiritual gifts, he positively encouraged the Corinthians to seek the gift of prophecy so that the church could be built up. Yet at the same time he exercised his apostolic authority; an authority far above that which he recognized as being operative in the prophetic gift in the Corinthian church. In so doing, Paul claimed to be as authoritative as the canonical prophets of the Old Testament.

In our first chapter we recalled Tommy Cooper's famous joke about the man who went into the bar and said 'Ouch' – because it was an iron bar. Just as that 'bar' has to be understood in context in order to make sense of the sentence, so we have to understand the words 'prophet' and 'prophecy' in context, or we will make a nonsense of what the Bible says. The fact that the same words are used to describe prophetic phenomena does not imply that the phenomena are always of similar character and authority.[1]

In the next chapter we must look more closely at

---

[1]'Words have histories as well as etymologies. The meaning of any given word in any given context depends at least as much upon the place and use of the word in that context as upon any supposed derivation.' C. Brown (ed.), *New International Dictionary of New Testament Theology*, vol. 1 (Grand Rapids: Zondervan; Exeter: Paternoster Press, 1975), p. 10.

apostles and prophets as the foundational people within the New Testament church.

For further thought and discussion

1. Why did Luke portray the apostles in Acts as the true successors of the classical prophetic tradition? What qualities and qualifications enabled them to be that?
2. What do the letters to the churches in Revelation 2 and 3 tell us about the apostles as prophets? How can we apply the message of these prophetic letters to today's church?
3. How did Paul deal with counterfeit apostolic prophecy (2 Thes. 1)? What does that teach us concerning those who make prophetic claims today?
4. Paul also recognized that there was a type of prophecy which was to be tested (1 Thes. 5:19–21). What might cause a prophecy of this type to fail the test?
5. If Agabus was wrong in details of prophecy, why was he not rejected as a false prophet? What is the difference between falsehood and fallibility?
6. Why is it so important to understand 'prophet' and 'prophecy' in context?

4/Apostles and prophets

n chapter 3 we saw that in the New Testament apostles are regarded as the true successors of the Old Testament canonical prophets. As the prophets were authoritative spokesmen for the covenant God of Israel, so Paul, for example, calls himself a minister of the new covenant (2 Cor. 3:6). The word 'apostle' means 'sent one', and the claim to possess a divine commission is central to the apostolic vocation (*cf*. Rom. 1:1; Gal. 1:1; Eph. 1:1; Mt. 10:1; Mk. 3:14). We have also noted that Luke in his presentation of the apostolic preaching in Acts demonstrates that the apostles are the true inheritors of the classical Old Testament prophetic tradition.

What is the difference?

What then do we make of the prophets of the New Testament church such as Agabus (Acts 11:28; 21:10) and the prophets of 1 Corinthians 12 – 14, *etc.*? We might well have assumed on initial encounter with the title 'prophet' in such passages that the word must have had a similar connotation to that found in the majority of Old Testament references to prophecy, namely to describe those who claimed to bring the very words of God to his people. On closer examination, however, we find that this proves not to be the case. While the apostles are connected with the classical Old Testament prophets, prophets in the New Testament church are never linked directly to them.

Why then were apostles not called prophets, and some other term found for those who did not claim a similar authority? It is likely that in popular usage 'prophet' did not convey adequately the sense of 'authoritative spokesman' at that time and was therefore not a suitable alternative to 'apostle'. The word was used in rabbinic literature to refer to those who could predict the future or who possessed supernatural insight, without any suggestion that they were being placed on a par with the canonical prophets.[1]

The letter to the Hebrews gives us a good example of the usage of 'apostle' and 'prophet'. Hebrews contains many references to Old Testament words and imagery. In our theology we are used to the idea of Jesus as prophet, priest and king. But while the writer to the Hebrews speaks of Jesus in kingly terms (Heb. 1:5–9) and refers to him as high priest (Heb. 3:1) he is never designated prophet in the letter. This is all the more remarkable because Hebrews begins: 'In the past God spoke to our forefathers through the *prophets* at many times and in various ways, but in these last days he has spoken to us by his Son . . .' (Heb. 1:1).

Clearly, the prophetic role of Jesus is assumed in these words; while God had spoken many times previously, he had now spoken decisively and fully through Jesus. Yet he is not called 'prophet'. In fact in Hebrews 3:1 we find Jesus designated as 'the *apostle* and high priest whom we confess'. The

[1]W. Grudem, *The Gift of Prophecy in 1 Corinthians* (Washington, DC: University Press of America, 1982), pp. 24–33.

writer then compares Jesus with Moses, the arche-typal *prophet* of the Old Testament tradition, but refuses to use the term to describe Christ. Though this might have been due to the fact that the principal theme of Hebrews is Jesus our high priest, the word 'prophet' was probably just not specific enough in New Testament times to convey the sense of absolute verbal authority. After all, the church had been launched at Pentecost with the promise that many, both men and women, would prophesy in fulfilment of Joel 2:28–29. The early church therefore needed another word to describe those who were channels of the oracles of God in their generation. 'Apostle' could convey that very well because, by definition, it meant those who had been sent out with an authoritative message to proclaim. As ambassadors for Christ they did not offer their own hunches but proclaimed the word of the Lord. And since 'apostle' was a new term, it could be used without confusion.

In addition, we have already noted from 1 Corinthians 14:37–38 that in a situation where a number of New Testament prophets were operating in a church Paul asserted his apostolic authority over the whole congregation, including the prophets, claiming that what he wrote was a command of the Lord. This shows that in the Corinthian church there were prophets who were not also apostles, although it does not rule out the possibility that in addition to exercising their distinctive apostolic role the apostles may well have functioned in ways similar to those prophets.

To summarize: the apostles were so designated because they were the authoritative messengers, commissioned by the risen Christ (1 Cor. 9:1), who proclaimed the word of the Lord in the same way as the canonical prophets of Old Testament fame. Those called 'prophets' in the New Testament churches were not comparable in authority and function to classical Old Testament prophets, but were subject to the authority of the message proclaimed by the apostles.

We have noted this already, exemplified most clearly in Paul's handling of the prophet Agabus in Acts 21 (see above, pp. 61–63). The apostles listened to what such prophets said, and, as Paul advised the Corinthians, weighed carefully their message before taking action. But they, like the church as a whole, might decide that God's will was not quite what the prophet had said! If there was any conflict caused by a prophetic resistance to the apostolic teaching, that was another matter. Then prophets in the church were reminded that the word of God originated with the apostles (1 Cor. 14:36). They should be eager to prophesy, but they should also ensure that all was brought under the judgment of the word of God revealed through Christ's ambassadors (2 Cor. 5:20).

Apostles and prophets in Ephesians

If the distinction between apostles and Christian prophets is so clear, we must ask why Paul seems to connect them in Ephesians 2:20 and 3:5, where we read:

> Consequently, you are no longer foreigners and aliens, but fellow-citizens with God's people and members of God's household, built on the foundation of the *apostles and*

74

prophets, with Christ Jesus himself as the chief cornerstone . . .

In reading this, then, you will be able to understand my insight into the mystery of Christ, which was not made known to men in other generations as it has now been revealed by the Spirit to God's holy *apostles and prophets*. (Eph. 2:19–20; 3:4–5)

As 'apostles and prophets' occurs twice within nine verses (2:19 – 3:5), it is natural to assume that Paul is using the words in the same way in both instances. But does he mean 'apostles and Old Testament prophets' or 'apostles and New Testament prophets'? Or could it be that the phrase refers to the one class, the apostles? Another possibility might be that Paul is not thinking about persons but about the message which came through them. In this way 'the foundation of the apostles and prophets' might be another way of speaking of Scripture as the record of the preaching and teaching of apostles and prophets which is the bedrock of the Christian church.

The last of these possibilities can be dealt with first. It is unlikely that Paul could have been thinking in such impersonal terms, since the chief component of the foundation is said to be 'Christ Jesus *himself*' (Eph. 2:20). The imagery is of the church as a great building with a superstructure built upon a solid base which, like any sound foundation, need not be laid again. Paul likens the members of the church to the building-blocks which the Ephesians would immediately have associated with the massive edifices of their own city, famous for its temple of Artemis, which was much bigger than the

Parthenon of Athens. They are to think of themselves as essential parts of the structure built on such firm foundations, with Christ Jesus himself being the cornerstone who holds it all together. It is the fact of their interconnectedness which Paul is teaching here, in encouraging unity in the church. The stress is on the fact that, like it or not, they are inseparably connected to one another and to Christ. The whole passage is about personal relationships among those who have found peace with God through Christ (Eph. 2:18–22). It was not just that their faith was based on the teaching *about* Jesus; it was that Jesus *himself* held the church together, aided and abetted by his associates, the apostles. In an amazing mixture of metaphors, Paul can refer not only to buildings but also to citizenship and family membership (Eph. 2:19) as indicative of their relationships as God's people. Of course, the teaching *about* Christ had been instrumental in introducing them into that new world of relationships. But as the plan of a building is to the final structure, so the teaching of Jesus and his apostles is to the church. A plan without a building is as pointless as doctrine without true fellowship in Christ. As the security of the upper storeys of a building depends on firm foundations, so the unity of the church depends on real relationships to fellow Christians and to Christ himself.

I might be tempted to go further into architectural imagery, as my primary academic study was in that field, but space forbids! We are left with the other three possibilities noted above, and we must deal with them in turn.

First of all, could Paul be thinking of the foundation metaphor as an illustration of the unique place of the Old Testament prophets and New Testament apostles in the unfolding of God's purposes? Surely any Christian might rightly feel connected with those great heroes of old, the founding fathers of faith? While that may be a worthy thought, it does not seem to explain 'apostles and prophets' here. This might seem surprising in view of the fact that we have already established the close kinship of classical Old Testament prophecy with the apostles whom Christ sent out as his ambassadors. But Paul seems to be saying something different in Ephesians.

There are a number of reasons for this. The whole passaage (Eph. 2:11 – 3:13) concerns how God has made a new beginning in establishing the church of Jesus Christ. The Gentile believers in Ephesus are reminded of their former alienation from the people of God, the Jews. Through the death of Jesus and faith in him they have been brought together. It is unlikely that this thought would be undergirded by reference to Old Testament prophecy, especially as no other representatives of the Jewish tradition are mentioned. In addition, Ephesians 3:5, quoted above, implies that 'apostles and prophets' are foundational in the New Testament church because of their reception of the revelation of the mystery of Christ, 'which was not made known to men in other generations'. Here 'apostles and prophets' are being set apart as in some sense distinctive from their forerunners, as those who had come to know Christ, in whom all the mysteries of God's purposes were consummated, including the amazing plan to unite Jew and Gentile in the body of Christ, the church.

Secondly, we must ask if Paul could be referring

to the apostles along with the Christian prophets such as Agabus and the Corinthian prophets. There is no doubt that in Ephesians 4:11 Paul distinguishes between apostles and prophets: 'It was he [Christ] who gave *some* to be apostles, *some* to be prophets, some to be evangelists, and some to be pastors and teachers.' Paul recognized that in the early church there were people with special ministries which distinguished them from other believers. They were key people in the upbuilding of the body of Christ. As we have seen, prophets could give valuable advice in directing the church, and bring encouragement, strength and comfort to God's people. Even if a believer had only once been given a prophetic insight which he or she had shared with the church, it could be crucial in the unfolding purposes of God. How much more, then, did God value those with a regular prophetic ministry?

In speaking of 'the foundation of the apostles and prophets' (Eph. 2:20), however, Paul seems to be speaking of a fixed and recognizable group of people who formed the basis of the church. In 1 Corinthians 14:1–19 Paul encourages his hearers to look for an increase in the numbers of those who prophesy in the church. But it is much more likely that Paul is speaking in Ephesians of a single, definable class of 'foundation-people' who were widely recognized as having a unique role in the establishing of the church, and whose numbers were clearly delimited.

Of course the term 'apostle' can be used in a wider sense than that. In the New Testament a number of people are called apostles who were not among the original band of eleven (plus Paul) who

78

had been personally commissioned by the risen Lord (1 Cor. 9:1). In such cases 'apostle' seems to mean 'missionary' or 'delegate', as in 2 Corinthians 8:23 ('representatives of the churches'), where the reference includes Titus. Andronicus and Junias are described as 'outstanding among the apostles' in Romans 16:7. This could mean that because they were among the early converts to Christianity (before Paul, as he notes) they were highly esteemed among the apostles. But it may indicate that they were well-known travelling preachers, and that 'apostle' just means missionary in the broader sense.

That usage is exceptional in Paul's letters, however, and has no bearing on our understanding of Ephesians 2 and 3, where 'apostles and prophets' clearly refers to apostles in the limited sense. Our final possibility is that 'apostles and prophets' refers to apostle-prophets – 'apostles-who-are-also-prophets'. This is a figure of speech called *hendiadys*, where two distinct words connected by a conjunction are used to express a single complex notion. In English this figure is often used, as in the phrase 'wife and mother' – a wife who is also a mother. The construction is also used widely in the Greek of the New Testament.[1] A good example is found in Ephesians 4:11, where 'pastors and teachers' are listed as essential to the upbuilding of the church. A pastor shepherds the flock by teaching; he is a pastor-who-is-also-a-teacher. There are over twenty Pauline examples where it is clear that hendiadys is being used to describe only *one* person or group.[2]

[1] *Ibid.*, pp. 97–101.
[2] *Ibid.*, p. 101; *cf.* D. Hill, *New Testament Prophecy* (London:

Ephesians 2:20 should be interpreted, therefore, as thinking of 'apostles and prophets' as one group. Along with Ephesians 3:5, where the phrase recurs, we have a way of describing the unique position of the apostles within the church of Jesus Christ. They are not only recipients of the 'mystery of Christ' (Eph. 3:4), a revelation from God which, among other things, makes known the amazing truth that through the gospel the Gentiles are heirs together with the Jews when they believe the promises of God fulfilled in Jesus Christ. The apostles are also prophets, in the New Testament sense. On that basis Paul is well able to pull rank (1 Cor. 14:36–38)!

This insight is enormously helpful in our understanding of prophecy in the New Testament. There are Christian prophets who function in the New Testament church, as we have noted in chapter 3. They are listed in Ephesians 4:11 as crucial to the establishing of the church. But they are subordinate, to the teaching of the apostles, and are not freelance! The apostles themselves also exercise a prophetic ministry, so there is no danger of the church being led astray.

We must therefore begin to ask more searching questions about the nature of New Testament prophecy as exercised by apostle-prophets and those who prophesied in the church. In chapter 7 we will try to summarize our findings regarding the form, content and function of New Testament

Marshall, Morgan & Scott, 1979), p. 139, where another viable interpretation is offered, based on hendiadys: 'They are apostles in that they are the authoritative witnesses to, indeed the representatives, of Jesus, and they are prophets by virtue of the fact that they are the authentic messengers and agents of the revelation they received.'

prophecy: how people prophesied, the kind of things they said, and what prophecy aimed to achieve in the life of the church.

But before we can do that two areas need to be studied. First, we need to look at the relationship between prophecy and preaching/teaching in the New Testament. There have been a number of attempts to suggest that the only continuing dimension of Christian prophecy is no more than an aspect of expository preaching, applied appropriately to the real situation of the church.[1] Secondly, we need to think about prophecy as revelation, because some might argue that if we classify prophecy as revelation, as Paul does, we are putting all prophecy on a par with the word of God which is now recorded in the New Testament. These two issues will be tackled in chapters 5 and 6 respectively.

For further thought and discussion

1. What does it mean to confess Christ as apostle of our faith (Heb. 3:1)? Why is it useful to compare Jesus with Moses, the supreme prophet of old?
2. In what way do we consider ourselves to be 'related' to the apostles? What is unique about their position in the family of God?
3. How should we react to modern prophets who contradict the apostolic teaching? How does 1 Corinthians 14:36–38 help us?

---

[1]*Cf.* D. Macleod, *The Spirit of Promise* (Tain: Christian Focus Publications, 1986).

5/Prophecy, preaching and teaching

We have already noted that Calvin thought of the office of teacher as being very similar in character to that of prophet, with exactly the same purpose (pp. 20–22). This view has been of enormous influence in the Reformed churches. It is interesting to note, however, that in the Authorized (King James) Version of the English Bible published in 1611, the Greek 'to prophesy' (*prophēteuō*) is never translated 'to preach', which is a different concept.[1] As we have seen, following Peter's sermon at Pentecost the apostles expected prophecy to be a common phenomenon in the church, and Paul encouraged the Corinthians to be eager to prophesy. Furthermore, Paul expected women to be among those who prophesied in church: 'every woman who prays or *prophesies* . . .' (1 Cor. 11:5).

Teaching/preaching

This is in marked contrast to the New Testament approach to teaching/preaching. James says: '*Not*

[1] E. Best, 'Prophets and Preachers', *Scottish Journal of Theology* 12 (1959), pp. 129–150. 'Exegesis of the OT, whether simply eschatological or both charismatic and eschatological, was the

many of you should presume to be teachers' (Jas. 3:1). Paul in his instructions to Timothy concerning the ordination of elders who engage in preaching and teaching says: *'Do not be hasty* in the laying on of hands' (1 Tim. 5:22). Coupled with that are Paul's guidelines about the qualities expected of those who teach, found in 1 Timothy 3:1–7 and Titus 1:5–9, which include the following qualities: 'able to *teach*' (1 Tim. 3:2) and able to 'encourage others by sound *doctrine*' (Tit. 1:9).

In addition, Paul's attitude to women and teaching is well known: *'I do not permit* a woman to teach or to have authority over a man; she must be silent' (1Tim. 2:12). Whatever this may indicate about Paul's attitude to women preachers – and there are different interpretations which seek to do justice to Paul's statement here while having reservations about many aspects of modern feminism[1] – of one thing we can be sure: Paul's attitude to women who prophesy is markedly different. (We shall look at this in more detail in chapter 9.)

It is no good, either, to appeal to a theory which once held sway, that there is a great difference in form and content between preaching and teaching in the New Testament. It was once believed that preaching (*kērygma*) described the proclamation of an outline of the gospel, in evangelism, and that teaching (*didachē*) involved doctrinal, moral and ethical instruction. When the apostles evangelized Jerusalem, the reaction noted by Luke in Acts 5:28 is significant: the Sanhedrin said, 'you have filled

---

primary province of the teacher', D. Aune, *Prophecy in Early Christianity and the Ancient Mediterranean World* (Grand Rapids: Wm B. Eerdmans, 1983), p. 345.

[1]For detailed discussion of this issue, see J. B. Hurley, *Man and Woman in Biblical Perspective* (Leicester: IVP, 1981), pp. 195–233.

Jerusalem with your *teaching*'. So we must agree with Michael Green when he says: 'Primitive evangelism was by no means mere proclamation and exhortation; it included able intellectual argument, skilful study of the scriptures, careful, closely-reasoned teaching, and patient argument.'[1]

The relation between prophecy and preaching

It is futile to link prophecy with exhortatory preaching in the hope that some aspect of preaching might be equated with prophecy. The two are quite distinct, while preaching and teaching overlap in many ways. This is further seen in Paul's words to Timothy: 'I give you this instruction in keeping with the *prophecies* once made about you, so that by following them you may fight the good fight' (1 Tim. 1:18) and 'Do not neglect your gift, which was given you through a *prophetic message* when the body of elders laid their hands on you' (1 Tim. 4:14). Timothy's gift concerned the teaching of the apostolic doctrine, as he was to devote himself to the public reading of Scripture, to preaching and teaching (1 Tim. 4:13). This is re-emphasized in Paul's 'famous last words' to Timothy, recorded in 2 Timothy 4:2–3: '*Preach* the Word; be prepared in season and out of season; correct, rebuke and encourage – with great patience and careful instruction. For the time will come when men will not put up with sound *doctrine*.' While preaching is clearly a matter of the proclamation of the apostolic teaching, prophecy is concerned with more existential affairs – what to

[1]M. Green, *Evangelism in the Early Church* (London: Hodder & Stoughton, 1970), p. 160.

do in specific circumstances and how to discern God's will.

Although we would be misguided always to equate prophecy with an aspect of preaching, it would also be wrong to exclude prophecy from what preachers might say. Involved in Timothy's preaching and teaching were to be correction, rebuke and encouragement (2 Tim. 4:2). This is remarkably similar to the prophetic purpose described by Paul in 1 Corinthians: 'But everyone who *prophesies* speaks to men for their strengthening, encouragement and comfort' (1Cor. 14:3). There is no doubt that much of preaching/teaching has a similar objective, and that it would be right to hope that many preachers would have prophetic insights which enable them to apply the word pointedly to the situations in which they operate. But that does not imply that all prophecy necessarily comes through those entrusted with the regular teaching of the word of God, as we shall see. Preachers may be prophetic, but not all who prophesy are preachers.

To summarize: while 'preaching' and 'teaching' overlap as words to describe the communication of church leaders in the New Testament, so that doctrine was proclaimed with the authority of the heralds of Jesus Christ, prophecy was distinctive in many ways. While preachers might prophesy, prophets were not necessarily preachers. While many could prophesy, few could preach and teach. While, for Paul, the exercising of authority through preaching was a man's job, prophecy could be engaged in by both men and women.[1]

[1]Discussion of 'words of knowledge and wisdom' can be found below, pp. 97–109.

For further thought and discussion

1. Have you ever considered a sermon to have been prophetic? In what way?
2. Why must we distinguish between prophecy and teaching? What is distinctive about Christian prophecy as described in the New Testament?

6/Prophecy as revelation

As we have noted in chapter 5, some interpreters have tried to subsume prophecy under the heading of preaching/teaching, so that New Testament prophecy has been thought of as no more than well-applied expository preaching. The same interpreters might, however, have difficulty with the idea of having women preachers! For that is the logical result of the equation if we take seriously Paul's instructions to women who prophesy (1 Cor. 11:5).

The relation between prophecy and revelation

Another area where problems have arisen is in Paul's reference to prophecy as 'revelation': 'And if a *revelation* comes to someone who is sitting down, the first speaker should stop. For you can all *prophesy* in turn . . .' (1 Cor. 14:30–31).

The argument goes like this. 'Revelation' (Gk. *apokalypsis*) is in the New Testament closely related to the inspiration of the apostles as communicators of the very words of God and in the Old Testament to the utterances of the classical prophets. Several references might be taken to support this view. We read that the prophet Nathan, in bringing a message from God to David about the building of a temple for God's glory, reported to David all the words of the *revelation* he had received (2 Sa. 7:17). The writer of Proverbs lamented that where there is no *revelation* the people cast off restraint (Pr. 29:18). Daniel received a *revelation* which involved a detailed vision concerning a great war which was yet to happen (Dn. 10:1–21a). Habakkuk was commanded to write down the *revelation* entrusted to him (Hab. 2:2). Simeon, who awaited the Messiah in Jerusalem, welcomed the baby Jesus as the one who would be 'a light for *revelation* to the Gentiles' (Lk. 2:32). Paul claimed, in his earliest letter, that the gospel he preached was not man-made, but that he had received it by *revelation* from Jesus Christ (Gal. 1:11–12). And of course the last book of the New Testament begins with the words 'The *revelation* of Jesus Christ ... to his servant John' (Rev. 1:1).

Revelation is accordingly a concept closely connected with the kind of absolute verbal authority which was claimed by Old Testament prophets and New Testament apostles. The argument therefore suggests that if revelation invariably implies verbal inspiration then prophecy must have been a form of communication which, whenever it occurred in the New Testament, always claimed to be the very words of God. If prophecy is revelation, it continues, then it must have been a phenomenon which was operative only during the days when Scripture was being written and gathered together; when the canon was completed there would have been no further need for it, as God was well able to guide his people through the Holy Spirit's application of the teaching of the word of God which was then fully available. Prophecy was either a means of bringing inspired words (some of which may have been incorporated in the New Testament) to the churches or it was a method of divine guidance which was needed during that interim period in which Scripture was becoming available.

Of course, it is absolutely correct to say that without 'revelation' there could be no prophecy, as Paul himself says in 1 Corinthians 14:30–31. It is the coming of a revelation which moves the prophet to speak. But does this necessarily mean 'the revealing of words from God to man'? Let us look at a few examples of how Paul uses the words 'reveal' and 'revelation', which occur thirty times in his letters.

In Philippians 3:15 Paul is encouraging his hearers to have a mature perspective in their Christian life, forgetting the past and pressing on towards heaven: 'And if on some point you think differently, that too God will *reveal* to you' (my translation). Here the NIV translates 'that too God will *make clear* to you'. Revelation in this case concerns the clarification of doctrine transmitted through Paul, not the revealing of some new truth. The idea is that some insight which has remained concealed to their understanding, whether it is central to Paul's argument or is only a lesser point, will become clarified in their minds.

In Romans 1:18 Paul begins his discourse on human sin and its consequences by saying: 'The wrath of God is being *revealed* from heaven against all the godlessness and wickedness of men who suppress the truth . . .' The wrath of God is not for Paul to be limited to the end of the world, but is seen in the abandonment of the wicked in their sins. They suppress the truth, not invariably because they have heard and rejected the word of God, but because they rebel against the truth about God which is clearly perceived in the created order (Rom. 1:19). That the wrath of God *is being* revealed (present continuous tense) further underlines Paul's point. This revelation is seen in the process of human history, as God lets man have what he persistently says he wants, with the resultant chaos of idolatry and immorality.

In Romans 1:18–32 the phrase 'God gave them over ...' (vv. 24, 26, 28) echoes throughout the passage describing the state in which sinful mankind exists in rebellion against the Creator. Just as God is in some sense revealed through the universe he has made, so also his nature and purposes are revealed through the process of human history. In both cases God has supplied further revelation in verbal form to explain something of the meaning of creation and of his mighty acts in history. And even sinful man, whether he likes it or not, is confronted by the revelation of God's wrath, just as he is deeply (if subconsciously) aware of God's eternal power and divine nature (Rom. 1:20). This is what theologians call *general* revelation: revelation which comes through nature and history but which needs to be qualified by *special* revelation, as recorded in Scripture. The main point for our purposes here is that 'revelation' is powerfully used by Paul in Romans 1 as a concept which need not imply absolute verbal authority.

In Ephesians 1:17 another use of 'revelation' is found in Paul's prayer: 'I keep asking that the God of our Lord Jesus Christ, the glorious Father, may give you the Spirit of wisdom and *revelation*, so that you may know him better.' This is not, surely, a prayer that the Ephesians might become channels of the very words of God, as Paul claimed to be. It was, rather, Paul's concern that they might enter more deeply into their relationship with God and discover more of the depths of his love. This is consistent with our understanding of human relationships and how they grow as we reveal to one another the secret thoughts and feelings within us. How much more, then, will the believer experience that kind of revelation as he grows to know God better.

In Matthew that kind of personal revelation is seen as central to the mission of Christ, where Jesus is quoted as saying:

> I praise you, Father, Lord of heaven and earth, because you have hidden these things from the wise and learned, and *revealed* them to little children ... No-one knows the Son except the Father, and no-one knows the Father except the Son and those to whom the Son chooses to *reveal* him. (Mt. 11:25–27)

There is no doubt that Jesus is speaking primarily about truths revealed through him and shared with his disciples, but these truths are intended to lead his people into a personal relationship in which the secrets of the Father's being, purposes and presence are increasingly made known. Because of that Jesus was able to continue with the incomparable words: 'Come to me, all you who are weary and burdened, and I will give you rest' (Mt. 11:28). This is the objective of God's revelation of himself, that man should be at rest as he lives in harmony with his Father, encouraged by his elder brother Jesus. That revelation should lead to rest proclaims powerfully that the New Testament can and does employ the notion of *apokalypsis* in terms of existential experience as well as an apt description of revealed truth in verbal form.

To summarize: revelation need not imply the revealing of words from God to man so that a message is proclaimed with absolute verbal authority. It could refer also to the clarification of a point of teaching which believers have already heard; it might be an awareness of what God is doing in the process of human history; it might be an insight into devotional matters which deepens one's experience of God. What classes such insights as 'revelation' is the appropriateness of the thought or the new awareness experienced in the lives of those who receive them, whether the matters unveiled are new to the prophet's thinking or old thoughts applied in a timely and relevant way. In 1 Corinthians revelation of that order is described as functioning in the church in Corinth.

In chapter 7 we want to ask what such revelation (prophecy) was like in the experience of those who gathered for worship. What form did it take, what content did it contain, what was the point of it, what was its function? But before we conclude these thoughts on revelation we have to ask why prophecy in Corinth was classed as revelation. (And we also need to look at what Paul calls 'words of wisdom and knowledge', phenomena which are often confused with prophecy.) This will enable us to appreciate more fully the form, content and function of Christian prophecy as experienced in the New Testament church.

Prophecy and revelation in Corinth

Paul lists revelation among the component parts of the worship in the church at Corinth. As in the Old Testament and synagogue worship, hymns and words of instruction were considered essential. The Jews used parts of the Psalms as hymns of worship, as is clear from the record of the Last Supper (Mt. 26:30). By the time Paul wrote 1 Corinthians it is likely that specifically Christian hymns were in circulation (it has been suggested, for example, that 1 Corinthians 13 and Philippians 2:5–11 may have begun life as hymns of praise in the church). Words of instruction were always central to synagogue worship, and it is likely that Paul adopted teaching patterns akin to what he had learnt in his rabbinic training.

As we have noted already, teaching (*didachē*) overlaps in many ways with preaching (*kērygma*). In the synagogue it was possible for any male Jew to be asked to read Scripture and comment upon it, as Jesus did in Luke 4:16–21 at Nazareth. Paul took advantage of that tradition many times in his travels, when he often went to the synagogue first to preach the gospel. (In Acts 13:13–15 we have an example of Paul being asked to speak in a synagogue following the reading of Scripture.) As the Corinthian church had been established as an offshoot from the synagogue (Acts 18:1–17), it is likely that Jewish traditions of worship had an important influence on the development of worship in the Christian church. Because of this we must avoid interpreting 1 Corinthians 14 through twentieth-century Western eyes, and instead allow ourselves to imagine (as far as is possible from the evidence)

93

the situation in that first-century worship service.

Unlike many services today, the form of worship in Corinth seems to have been relatively unstructured. Participation by all members of the church was encouraged so long as it was done in a fitting and orderly way (1 Cor. 14:40). But not everybody was like Paul, who seemed to exercise many spiritual gifts which he could contribute in worship. He was concerned to teach that not all gifts were for everyone and that there were different ways of serving the Lord (1 Cor. 12:5), the same Holy Spirit manifesting his presence in different ways through the believers for the common good (1 Cor. 12:7).

It is interesting that in two sections where Paul refers to the exercise of spiritual gifts teaching is to the fore: 'To one there is given through the Spirit the message [*logos*] of wisdom, to another the message [*logos*] of knowledge by means of the same Spirit . . . (1 Cor. 12:8, see pp. 97–109), and, 'When you come together, everyone has a hymn, or a teaching [*didachē*; 'word of instruction', NIV], a revelation, a tongue or an interpretation' (1 Cor. 14:26, my translation). Such teaching would have taken the form of a reading from Scripture (Old Testament) or from an apostolic letter, followed by exposition or exhortation. Perhaps collections of some of Jesus' sayings were in circulation among the churches at that time, prior to the compilation of what were later termed the Gospels.

While it may well have been possible for any male member of the church to offer a word of teaching, it is likely that those whom God had called to exercise a teaching ministry would have been recognized and given priority. One of the reasons elders (overseers) were appointed was because they showed aptitude in that direction, as we have already noted (1 Tim. 3:2; Tit. 1:9).

On the basis of these observations, it would be unwise to think of worship in Corinth (at least in terms of what Paul would have encouraged) as a free-for-all. Yet it seems from 1 Corinthians that things *had* got out of hand and spontaneity was being stressed so that regular, less dramatic contributions were considered of lower value. Tongues, which Paul considered valuable mostly in private devotions (1 Cor. 14:4a, 18–19), were being used without interpretation in worship meetings. Prophets were also speaking too often, and Paul had to limit such contributions to two or three (1 Cor. 14:29) and stress that all prophecy was subject to the granting of revelations (1 Cor. 14:30), not merely to the whim of prophets.

Following the praise and teaching, it seems that prophetic insights might be shared which enhanced the instruction given and encouraged the believers (1 Cor. 14:31). Such contributions would focus upon the practical outworking of what was taught; what God wanted them to do about it, and whether he was with them in what they were presently doing. It might, for example, clarify teaching already received, make the church aware of what was happening in the world around them, or invite the believers to enter more deeply into their experience of God in Christ.

In practical terms we might think of this as discussion after the sermon. The discussion in which the prophets engaged was with a view to active obedience to the teaching received, and their insights were to be carefully considered by the whole congregation, whether they remained silent or took part in the discussion which followed.

It has been conjectured by many that the picture of prophetic utterance in 1 Corinthians 14:29–33 implies that such prophecy was always spontaneous and unrehearsed, and that the 'revelations' received were thoughts that the prophets had not previously entertained. This seems to be necessary if revelation means the *unveiling* of something previously hidden, but surely a long-held opinion might become a revelation if it was shared at the appropriate time. In the discussions we often see on television, for example, one contributor may feel that the right time has come to make a point he has thought of before and which he now (spontaneously) considers appropriate to contribute. The 'unveiling' is not of a new insight *per se*, but of its application to the particular discussion, so he interrupts another participant who may be in midflight! Similarly, prophecy is termed revelation not because the insights communicated are necessarily flashes of inspiration, but because they are appropriate to the situation at that time. Prophecy of this kind brings the *now-word* which offers insights into how God views the real situation from his perspective and points the church in a particular direction so that the teaching lives in the experience of believers, both individually and as a fellowship.

Another conjecture which is unhelpful is that such prophecy involved a revelation which came only to the individual prophet rather than to others in the congregation – and that it was always a new insight rather than a comment on what a previous prophet may have said or an expression of what the rest of the congregation may have been thinking. As the whole church engaged in the weighing of prophecies, however, it is most unlikely that no other member of the congregation ever had similar thoughts. In fact the possibility of confirming such insights as valid suggests that prophets may well have made public what many others were thinking to themselves. How often in response to preaching, for example, do people sometimes remark that the preacher seemed to know what they were thinking, that the message was 'for them'?

While it may be unwise to speculate too much about the nature of prophecy as revelation in 1 Corinthians, one thing is clear. The Greek words used for 'revelation' and 'reveal' always describe insights which are of divine origin and which enable Christians to know something from the perspective of the kingdom of God. It is a foretaste of the full unveiling of God's secrets which will take place at the day of Christ's return. Yet revelation is not limited to knowledge about that eschatological event, or even in a more general way to knowledge about things to come. Revelation takes place when a believer comes to see himself, the church and the world from a kingdom perspective.[1] Then in some fresh way we see ourselves as God sees us. In Corinth such insights could be shared by two or three prophets with those who gathered for worship.

Words of wisdom and knowledge

In addition to the phenomenon of prophecy as

[1]W. Grudem, *The Gift of Prophecy in 1 Corinthians* (Washington, DC: University Press of America, 1982), pp. 129–130.

97

revelation in Corinth, the church experienced 'words of wisdom and knowledge'. While these are not strictly related to prophecy as revelation, they are often treated as such in popular works, and seen as the spontaneous revelation of certain insights. We have suggested that such 'words' were part of the teaching which was given to the church by those whom God had called to expound the apostolic doctrine. We came to this conclusion because in the list of spiritual gifts noted in 1 Corinthians 12:8–10, no specific mention is made of teaching, while in the second list in the same chapter (vv. 28–30) teaching appears high on the agenda. While Paul is not intending to be exhaustive in either list, but is emphasizing, first, the variety of gifts given by the one Spirit and, secondly, the relative importance of various gifts, it is most unlikely that he would have entirely omitted teaching from the first list.

'Wisdom' and 'knowledge'

The *logos sophias* (word of wisdom) and *logos gnōseōs* (word of knowledge) are more likely to have been aspects of the teaching ministry than momentary revelatory insights. In 1 Corinthians 1:18–2:10 Paul associates the idea of *wisdom* with the preaching of Christ crucified. Paul speaks of 'God's secret wisdom' (1 Cor. 2:7) as being his plan to save sinners by the crucifixion of Jesus Christ. Wisdom is about the practical application of principles. God's wisdom – his way of doing things – is totally different from what man would do if left to his own resources. Christ can therefore be called 'wisdom from God' (1 Cor. 1:30), a wisdom made known through the teaching of the gospel: 'we speak of God's secret wisdom, a wisdom that has been hidden and that God destined for our glory before time began. None of the rulers of this age understood it, for if they had, they would not have crucified the Lord of glory' (1 Cor. 2:7–8). Part of the teaching ministry, therefore, is to expound the mystery of God's wisdom, to convince those who hear that God's ways, while they are not ours, truly reflect his nature. God's wisdom is consistent and logical, in other words, despite our inability to grasp the principles of his will by our own unaided efforts. Because of this we need teaching about a wisdom which until we receive the gospel is beyond our ken (*cf*. Is. 55:8).

Similarly, *knowledge* must be understood in context. Today a *word of knowledge* is often thought of as a form of extra-sensory perception in which details about the situation of another are revealed to the thoughts of believers, often in counselling or healing encounters.[1] In a healing meeting the leader may say that there is a person with a certain disability who should come forward, or in one-to-one counselling a pastor may understand, supernaturally, the cause of his counsellee's problem. Such flashes of insight are generally called 'words of knowledge' in modern usage. We would be wrong to deny that such things can and do happen – and not always in specifically Christian contexts (in fact the ability to read minds and predict the future has been observed in many religious

[1]J. Wimber, *Power Healing* (London: Hodder & Stoughton, 1986), p. 278: 'Word of knowledge: A spiritual gift through which God reveals facts about a situation for which a person had no previous knowledge (1 Cor. 12:8).' See Appendix 2 (c), below, pp. 206–207.

and secular traditions, and not all can be discarded as spurious) – but it is quite mistaken to label such insights as 'words of knowledge'.

That this is so can be demonstrated by reference to a concordance. First of all, we need to examine Paul's use of *logos* ('word'). Paul often speaks of the *word of God* when referring to the message he preached and about which he wrote (Rom. 9:6; 1 Cor. 14:36; 2 Cor. 2:17; 4:2; Phil. 1:14; Col. 1:25; 1 Thes. 2:13; 1 Tim. 4:5; 2 Tim. 2:9). This word is described as the *word of faith* (Rom. 10:8), the *word of truth* (Eph. 1:13) and the *word of life* (Phil. 2:16). In all these cases Paul is referring to his activity as a preacher of God's message. Let us look at them in more detail.

God's 'word'

In Romans 9:6 Paul is referring to the fact that the majority of his fellow Jews have rejected Jesus as Messiah, but suggests: 'It is not as though *God's word* has failed.' He then goes on to show that what has happened is consistent with the plan of God as revealed in Scripture. Again, in 1 Corinthians 14:36 Paul challenges the claims of those who believed themselves to be spiritually gifted as prophets and yet were not fully submitted to the apostolic teaching: 'Did the *word of God* originate with you? Or are you the only people it has reached?' Here the word is a message which has been communicated by the apostles as they reached out to more and more people. At that time there were many travelling preachers with a message to sell, so Paul has to put the record straight when in 2 Corinthians 2:17; 4:2 he says this to those who might classify him among such

100

spiritual 'peddlers': 'Unlike so many, we do not peddle the *word of God* for profit ... Rather, we have renounced secret and shameful ways; we do not use deception, nor do we distort the *word of God.*'

God's word was to Paul a coherent whole which had to be presented in a balanced way in order to convey the whole truth. Under pressure, preachers might be tempted to miss out parts of the message to avoid trouble, so in his diary notes of his first Roman imprisonment we have this interesting comment in Philippians 1:14: 'Because of my chains, most of the brothers in the Lord have been encouraged to speak the *word of God* more courageously and fearlessly.' It was Paul's self-awareness as an apostle of Jesus Christ that drove him to write with passion, during that same imprisonment, the further comment which we find in Colossians 1:25: 'I have become [the church's] servant by the commission God gave me to present to you the *word of God* in its fulness'. Paul goes on to say that God's word involved the revelation of the mystery of 'Christ in you, the hope of glory' (Col. 1:27). Then he says: 'We proclaim him, admonishing and teaching everyone with all wisdom, so that we may present everyone perfect in Christ' (Col. 1:28).

Paul thought of *the word* as a full and complete message which had to be taught with all the authority invested in the ambassadors of Christ. It was a message which had to be welcomed and accepted by those who heard it if it was to do them any good and produce in them the maturity of life and character which Christ alone could bring. So in 1 Thessalonians 2:13 Paul says: 'And we also

101

thank God continually because, when you received the *word of God*, which you heard from us, you accepted it not as the word of men, but as it actually is, the *word of God*, which is at work in you who believe.'

Anything contrary to the teaching of God's word was to be rejected, including any rules and regulations which might appear to be pious but which were alien to scriptural teaching. Some might come along and forbid marriage or the eating of certain foods, but, Paul retorted in 1 Timothy 4:4–5, 'nothing is to be rejected if it is received with thanksgiving, because it is consecrated by the *word of God* and prayer'. In other words marriage and God-given food sources were not to be despised, because God had clearly indicated in his word that they were special gifts from himself to his world. To enjoy these gifts was part of a holistic lifestyle which Paul considered to be based on the whole word of God.

Paul had supreme confidence in the efficacy of the message which he delighted to call the *word of God*. Even in his final imprisonment, not long before his execution, he shared with Timothy his feelings about being chained as a common criminal for the sake of the gospel: 'But *God's word* is not chained' (2 Tim. 2:9). The message which he proclaimed was at work in the lives of those who had received it, and would not return void of effect (*cf.* Is. 55:11).

All this serves to illustrate how Paul used *logos* to describe a coherent message (in full or in part) rather than a timely insight into a particular situation. God's word was pre-eminent to Paul because it was *God's* and not man's, and because it was a *logos*, a message which gave a coherent explanation of God and his world, consummated in Christ.

We are not surprised to find that word being described as the *word of faith* (Rom. 10:8), the message which encourages people to place their trust in Christ for salvation; the *word of truth* (Eph. 1:13), the message which deals with things as they really are in a reliable and authoritative way; and the *word of life* (Phil. 2:16), the message which is living and offers eternal life to those who receive it.

Yet faith, truth and life, while aptly describing the word of God, do not exhaust all the epithets that might be applied to the *logos*. Through the word of God come faith, truth and life, as do *wisdom* and *knowledge* (1 Cor. 12:8). It is significant that the NIV translates *logos sophias* and *logos gnōseōs* as '*message* of wisdom' and '*message* of knowledge'. In other words the *logos of wisdom* describes the word of God as proclaiming God's wise ways of dealing with people which are not our ways. When such a word is brought to the assembled believers it demonstrates that God's wisdom is clearly seen in the gospel and seeks to apply God's way of doing things to the life of the church. Without the word of wisdom the church would operate purely in terms of human methods and plans. Clearly we need to recover that awareness of the whole teaching of God's word if we are to move forward in God's will as individuals and congregations.

The word of knowledge

The *logos of knowledge* is not as simple to define. One reason for this is that 'knowledge' seems to have been a slogan in Corinth, something which a group of the believers claimed to possess. In

1 Corinthians, therefore, some references to knowledge have overtones which speak more of the Corinthians' own specialized use of the term than of Paul's understanding of *gnōsis* ('knowledge'). Some have suggested that this 'in-group' was the beginning of a movement which was later called 'Gnosticism' because it claimed to possess an esoteric knowledge which would illuminate initiates as no other teaching could, in a way similar to that claimed by modern Freemasonry.

Be that as it may, many times in his letters Paul explains what true knowledge is according to his gospel: 'I myself am convinced, my brothers, that you yourselves are ... complete in *knowledge*, and competent to instruct one another' (Rom. 15:14). This suggests that knowledge may be imparted and that it involves propositions which need to be taught. Such knowledge, however, is meant to lead believers into the experience of that which they learn. In Scripture knowledge often has the sense of knowing another personally. Paul speaks of knowledge in that way: 'And I pray that you, being rooted and established in love, may have power, together with all the saints, to grasp how wide and long and high and deep is the love of Christ, and to *know* this love that surpasses *knowledge* ...' (Eph. 3:17–19). In other words the love of Christ is so great that it cannot be fully known, but it can be experienced in a personal way despite the limitations of our understanding. Yet the existential knowing of Christ is closely related to the exposition of the word of God. Paul reminds us of the importance of this in Colossians, which was written at about the same time as Ephesians:

We have not stopped praying for you and asking God to fill you with the *knowledge* of his will ... [in order that you may grow] in the *knowledge* of God ...

My purpose is that they may be encouraged in heart and united in love, so that they may have the full riches of complete understanding, in order that they may *know* the mystery of God, namely, Christ, in whom are hidden all the treasures of wisdom and *knowledge*. I tell you this so that no-one may deceive you ...

... you have taken off your old self with its practices and have put on the new self, which is being renewed in *knowledge* in the image of its Creator (Col. 1:9–10; 2:2–4; 3:9–10).

For Paul, knowledge was not just head-knowledge, although he believed in teaching the truths of the word of God. To know the truth is to know Christ as a living person; to know the truth is to know oneself as a child of God. As Calvin aptly began his great treatise on the Christian religion: 'Without knowledge of self there is no knowledge of God.'[1] Unless we accept the truth about ourselves and live in the light of that reality we cannot hope to appreciate who God is and how to form a relationship with him. This reflects Paul's dynamic use of the word *gnōsis*; it is knowledge about the being and purposes of God, and of ourselves, which draws us into self-understanding and communion with the Creator.

Paul's concern that his hearers would grow in

---

[1] J. Calvin, *Institutes of the Christian Religion*, tr. F. L. Battles, ed. J. T. McNeill (Philadelphia: Westminster Press, 1960), vol. I, p. 35.

knowledge of God and themselves was a very practical one. Through growth in knowledge they would learn the principles of God's will, which is 'good, pleasing and perfect' (Rom. 12:2). They would grow in love for each other and would be protected from the influence of false teachers (Col. 2:2–4). They would know Christ and the power of his resurrection, sharing in his sufferings (Phil. 3:10), so that, as with Paul, everything would pale into insignificance in comparison with 'the surpassing greatness of knowing Christ Jesus my Lord' (Phil. 3:8).

It is not surprising, therefore, that when Paul lists the spiritual gifts which God has given his church for the upbuilding of the body of Christ, to the fore are 'the message [*logos*] of wisdom' and 'the message [*logos*] of knowledge' (1 Cor. 12:8). He considered the teaching of God's word to be the primary ministry which the church required. If the message was not proclaimed, expounding God's wisdom and knowledge, then everything else was pointless.[1]

---

[1] Such 'messages' need not always be thought of as sermons or lectures, but might be brief words of teaching following a short quotation of Scripture. An example of this is found in the morning meeting tradition of the Christian Brethren. Such a message is *logos* if it presents a truth or truths as part of the whole gospel, and not merely as an isolated insight into existential affairs. A New Testament example might be Paul's word to the Philippian jailer: 'Believe in the Lord Jesus Christ, and you will be saved' (Acts 16:31; *cf*. Rom. 10:9). This is based on the apostolic proclamation as a whole, yet focuses upon the particular need of the people in question. It invites the hearers to place their faith in Christ, in mind and heart. Such brief words could be called 'words of faith' (Rom. 10:8). Similarly, a 'word of knowledge' might be a brief message encouraging the knowledge of God or human existence, in mind and heart.

'Words of knowledge'

We have spent some time on this issue because it has become controversial in recent times. In chapter 10 we will apply this understanding to the claims of those who think of 'words of knowledge' in a different way. Suffice it to say that there is no basis in Paul's teaching for thinking of a word of knowledge as a spontaneous insight into the physical, mental or spiritual condition of another person at a particular point in time. Paul would never have used the words 'word' or 'knowledge' in that sense. While such insights may be possible, it is unwise to suggest that they are of fundamental importance in the ministry of the church because 'words of knowledge' are distinctive gifts of the Spirit. They are not mentioned directly by Paul in his references to spiritual gifts, and it is quite misleading to interpret 1 Corinthians 12:8 in this way.

It is possible, however, that the phenomenon described as a 'word of knowledge' is indeed *an aspect* of the prophetic gift. The account of Jesus' meeting with the woman at the well of Samaria (Jn. 4:1–42) is often cited as an example of this kind of thing, where Jesus was able to know intimate details about the woman's personal life. Recognizing Jesus to be a prophet (Jn. 4:19), she told her friends: 'He told me everything I ever did' (Jn. 4:39). In view of the fact that such insights seem to have been important to John's *Christology* (*i.e.* to his understanding of who Jesus really is) – note that the result of the incident was the confession 'this man really is the Saviour of the world' (Jn. 4:42) – it is doubtful whether Jesus'

107

supernatural insight should be equated with Christian prophecy.

Another example from John's Gospel, Jesus' encounter with Nathanael (Jn. 1:47–51), also reveals Jesus' amazing knowledge of people. In response to his question, 'How do you know me?', Jesus said to Nathanael that he had seen him under a fig-tree immediately prior to Philip's invitation to come and meet the Messiah. Nathanael's stunned response was, 'Rabbi, you are the Son of God; you are the King of Israel' (Jn. 1:49). In Corinth, thirty years later, prophecy in the church could elicit a similar sense of wonder. It could have the effect of exposing personal secrets and led unbelievers or enquirers to believe that God really was present in the worship service (1 Cor. 14:25). This may have been akin to what recent writers have called 'words of knowledge', but it would be unwise to be too dogmatic, so slender is the evidence for this aspect of prophecy.

While such experiences might convince people that God really was speaking to their personal need, it was not necessary to receive such prophetic words in order to come to faith in Christ as the Son of God. What was fundamental was the message of Christ crucified, the power of God to those who were being saved (1 Cor. 1:18), a message preached not with wise and persuasive oratory, but with a demonstration of the Spirit's power, despite the natural weakness and timidity of the preachers (1 Cor. 2:4–5). That demonstration was seen principally in powerful preaching which the Spirit brought home to the consciences of those who heard (1 Thes. 1:5), producing deep conviction.

Having dealt in this chapter with prophecy as revelation, and with associated issues, in chapter 7 let us think further about what prophecy was like in the Corinthian church, and what it was for.

For further thought and discussion

1. Think of occasions when you have experienced the kind of revelation described by Paul in Philippians 3:15, when the teaching of God's word has been made clear in your own mind after a struggle for understanding. How did you react?
2. In what ways do you see the wrath of God being revealed in today's world through the historical process (*cf.* Rom. 1:18–32)?
3. Have you found your relationship with God growing as you personally encounter him through Christ? In what ways would you say that experience was a revelation?
4. Do you feel happy at the thought of worship services where there is an element of spontaneity and unpredictability?
5. If God grants revelation in the manner described in questions 1–3 above, why should such insights be kept to oneself? When would it be appropriate to share valuable insights with other believers in your church? If it is not possible in corporate worship, what about small groups or discussion times? And what about leaders' meetings?
6. Why is it unwise to think of 'words of knowledge' as John Wimber does? (For his understanding, see p. 99, note.)

7/Christian prophecy—How? What? and Why?

To recapitulate: in the New Testament, prophetic phenomena can be divided into two classes. First, there is the absolutely authoritative prophecy exercised by the apostles and their associates who, like the classical prophets of the Old Testament, claimed that their message communicated the actual words of God to the church and, through the church, to the world. This kind of prophecy, much of which was recorded in the Scriptures of the New Testament, formed a unique and unrepeatable foundation, along with the teaching of Jesus, for the body of Christ.

The title 'apostle' was given to the messengers of Jesus because it reflected their status as ambassadors for Christ, proclaiming teaching which they had received either from him during his earthly ministry or through the Holy Spirit following his exaltation. Although the gospel writers Mark and Luke were not apostles in the limited sense of the term (in that we have no evidence that they were personally commissioned by the risen Lord before his ascension, or, like Paul, by extraordinary revelation) their prophetic writings, which were accepted as authoritative along with the writings of

Matthew, John, Paul and Peter, reflect their close relationship to Peter (who influenced Mark) and Paul (Luke's mentor). In addition, the letter to the Hebrews may have been written by an associate of Paul such as Barnabas or Apollos.

As a foundation is laid before a building is erected, so God began again with Jesus and his apostles. All Christians trace their origins back to them, and to the teaching they proclaimed. The church, like a well-constructed building, is soundly based on foundations which cannot be, and need not be, relaid. And Jesus himself, the absolutely unique Son of God, holds it all together as chief cornerstone. This he does by furnishing the church with those who will build up the people of God through the teaching of the prophetic writings entrusted to them.

Secondly, there is clear evidence that the early church recognized prophetic activity which made no such claims to being the very word of God. Such prophecy, which we have in this book called New Testament prophecy or Christian prophecy, did not seek to communicate the *logos* (word) of God, the apostolic message which focused on the person and work of Jesus Christ and offered a coherent explanation of reality, physical and spiritual, with Jesus at the centre of all things. Christian prophecy is not to be confused with the preaching and teaching of that *logos*, which was a distinctive ministry which the Holy Spirit raised up for the upbuilding of the body. It was through the preaching of that message that people found faith in Christ and a living knowledge of God. That touched their thinking, actions and emotions, and transformed them by the power of the Spirit into members of the body of Christ who increasingly reflected the character of Jesus and his lifestyle of service.

Yet the church was not living in a time-capsule, unrelated to the world of the day in which it existed. The church had to know what to do with the message it held so dear, who among its members were to be deployed for certain tasks, and where they were to serve. It had to know if it was being effective or effete, and assess whether, individually and as congregations, Christians were pleasing to God or needing to receive his rebuke. In addition, the church had to relate its message to the contemporary situation and understand what God was trying to say through historical events. In all of this, prophetic insights were to be subject to the overall authority of the word of God as revealed in Old Testament Scripture and apostolic teaching, and were never to be treated as oracles of God, but as divine promptings which might not have been perfectly picked up by those who received them. So they were to be tested and weighed by the church, and only what was judged to be truly God's will was to be accepted or acted upon.

It is not clear whether Christian prophecy of the type outlined above, which, as we have noted, is described in Acts, 1 Thessalonians and 1 Corinthians, is to be distinguished from the phenomenon of Pentecost and the related experiences which Luke records in Acts. There, prophecy seems to be described as a mighty sign of the presence of God, where no clear direction is received other than a general confirmation that God really is at work among his people, and that the last days have come in which many of God's people, men and women, will prophesy as a witness to the fact that the Holy Spirit has been poured out. It is doubtful if Luke or Paul, who saw such phenomena at Ephesus (Acts 19:1–7), considered that similar manifestations would be regularly experienced in the life of the churches. We noted earlier that it seemed to be comparable to the prophecy described in Numbers 11, when Moses' elders burst forth spontaneously into prophetic speech. But they did not do so again, as the record reminds us. It was a mighty sign of their entering a new phase in the unfolding of God's purposes, and not the beginning of a regular prophetic ministry. It may well be that the possibility of such extraordinary Christian prophecy was not ruled out by Luke and Paul. But that, as we have noted (pp. 63–70), is quite different from the attitude to prophetic activity which we find in 1 Corinthians 12 – 14, where Paul actively encourages the church in Corinth to seek the prophetic gift as vital to the ongoing work.

It is to Acts and 1 Corinthians 12 – 14 that we must turn for details about the form, content and function of Christian prophecy as it was expected to be exercised in a regular way in the life and worship of the church. By *form* we mean, What was prophecy like? How did prophets present their insights? By *content* we mean, What kind of things did they say? What subjects did they address? By *function* we mean, What was the purpose of Christian prophecy? What did it achieve that other types of communication did not?

The form and content of Christian prophecy

From the evidence of Christian prophecy in the

113

New Testament, it is impossible to discern whether prophets presented their insights by means of formulae or via standard patterns of speech.[1] The letters to the churches in Revelation 2 and 3 should not be taken as examples of how prophets might address congregations, despite the fact that the chorus, 'He who has an ear, let him hear what the Spirit says to the churches,' echoes several times. This is not an example of the kind of prophecy which we find in 1 Corinthians, because it claims an authority similar to the classical Old Testament prophets, who proclaimed 'Thus says the LORD.' It reflects instead the teaching of Jesus found in Matthew 11:13–15: 'For all the Prophets and the Law prophesied until John. And if you are willing to accept it, he is the Elijah who was to come. *He who has ears, let him hear.*' Jesus called his hearers to listen carefully to John the Baptist because he was the last of the line of prophets who prepared the way for the Messiah. Nowhere in the New Testament are Christian prophets such as those in 1 Corinthians compared to John or Elijah. We would therefore not expect them to address the churches with such a self-awareness of absolute verbal authority. We would not expect them to have presented their insights in the first person, as if God were speaking personally to the gathering of believers, as was sometimes the habit of classical prophets in the Old Testament.

There is, however, one example of a prophet in the New Testament who prefaced his words with

---

[1]'Christian prophecy produced no distinctive speech forms which would have been readily identifiable as prophetic speech,' D. Aune, *Prophecy in Early Christianity and the Ancient Mediterranean World* (Grand Rapids: Wm B. Eerdmans, 1983), p. 231.

114

'The Holy Spirit says . . .'. That is quoted of Agabus in Acts 21:11, where he predicted Paul's imminent capture with these words: 'The Holy Spirit says, "In this way the Jews of Jerusalem will bind the owner of this belt and will hand him over to the Gentiles."' This confirmed that God's will was for Paul to go up to Jerusalem, which he did after much discussion with Luke and his companions who tried to dissuade him. Yet when Paul got to Jerusalem things did not work out quite as Agabus had predicted. The mob in the temple tried to kill him (Acts 21:27–32) and the Romans intervened so that Paul was not beaten up. Then they (*not* the Jews) bound him with chains, which later proved an embarrassment because Paul was a Roman citizen (Acts 22:29).

It was the same Agabus who earlier in Acts had predicted a famine which actually happened, as Luke records (Acts 11:28–30): 'One of [the prophets], named Agabus, stood up and through the Spirit predicted that a severe famine would spread over the entire Roman world' (11:28). By contrast with Acts 21, his actual words are not quoted, but we may assume that his hearers understood him to have been prompted by the Holy Spirit to say what he did.

From this two things may be observed. First, Agabus was clearly respected as one whose track-record as a prophet was good. He had encouraged the church in Antioch to provide help for the church in Jerusalem during a severe famine. His prophecy was proved to be accurate, although it seems he never claimed to have details about the exact timing of events. Luke records parenthetically that the famine did occur, during

115

the reign of Claudius, who was Emperor at that time and continued in power for a further ten years or so. Their response was immediate, and Barnabas and Saul were sent off with gifts to Judea.

Secondly, the same Agabus is portrayed as being prompted by the Spirit to speak a word of prophecy to Paul at a later time, perhaps fifteen years after the Antioch experience. Yet, while he was in tune with the general thrust of what the Holy Spirit was saying (*i.e.* Paul was going to be incarcerated by the Romans), Agabus was wrong about the details.

This suggests that Christian prophets like Agabus felt compelled to share what they believed the Spirit was impressing upon them. They might even say that the Spirit had so moved them. Yet in the end what they said was open to discussion and evaluation. It was offered as part of the process of discerning God's will for the church and its leaders in specific situations. Apart from the accounts concerning Agabus there are no indications that prophecy was recognizable by the use of certain formulae or words of introduction. In some cases prophecy is mentioned without any further qualification than that certain persons prophesied (*cf.* Acts 19:6, 'they spoke in tongues and prophesied').

In 1 Corinthians we can glean pieces of information about the form of prophecy in the church, but we would be unwise to speculate too much. One such snippet concerns the way women were to participate in prophecy, and mentions men in passing, too: 'Every man who prays or prophesies with his head covered dishonours his head. And every woman who prays or prophesies with her head uncovered dishonours her head . . .' (1 Cor.

116

11:4–5). As we shall see in chapter 8, however, this is not so much about the form of prophecy as it is about the attitude of prophets. It certainly does not teach that men and women must dress in a particular way in order to prophesy!

What we can say with confidence about prophecy in Corinth is that it was addressed to the people who gathered in worship and was intelligible. It was not an ecstatic outburst in which the prophet was unaware of his surroundings or caught up in some trance-like state. Prophets were quite under control, unlike the Delphic oracles who were thought to act as mouthpieces for gods like Apollo in ancient Greece. We can see from 1 Corinthians 14:30 that prophets were not under some compulsion to burst forth into prophecy. They were quite able to stop what they were saying in order to let another contribute, so that each could prophesy in turn. The work of the Holy Spirit ensured that prophets could speak in a restrained and orderly way (1 Cor. 14:32). The result of the prophetic word was not disturbance, but peace, if prophets were functioning properly (1 Cor. 14:33). Those who heard understood what was said (1 Cor. 14:29) and prophecies brought understanding and encouragement (1 Cor. 14:31). If the hearers were able to grasp what was being said, it is likely that the prophets themselves understood what they were saying, even if they did not see all the implications of it (*cf*. Jn. 12:49–50; 1 Pet. 1:10–12). The group of prophets who contributed at any one time were well aware of their surroundings (1 Cor. 14:30) and were not 'spaced out' and detached from reality. They were aware of what others were saying and could 'butt in' to add to the discussion.

The disorder which Paul criticizes in 1 Corinthians 14:33 does not imply a mêlée of ecstatic outbursts, but that so many believers were keen to contribute that disorder resulted. The underlying problem in Corinth was a spirit of competition, which Paul tackles many times in the letter, whether it be competing over favourite preachers (1 Cor. 1:10–17) or over spiritual gifts (1 Cor. 12:1–31, *etc.*). There was also some disagreement over the participation of women in worship (1 Cor. 14:33b–35), an issue which we will deal with in chapter 8. But there is no hint that Paul was trying to correct a church which had become dominated by the emotional ravings of frenzied women! He was concerned that everything should be done in a fitting and orderly way (1 Cor. 14:40), so that the church, gathered for worship, would be upbuilt. Prophecy was important in that. While we cannot discern any particular form in which prophecy was presented to the church, we can summarize the principles involved by referring to the key verses of 1 Corinthians 14.

1. 'But everyone who prophesies speaks to men for their strengthening, encouragement and comfort' (1 Cor. 14:3)

In other words it was offered as a positive contribution to the ongoing work of building up the church. While this might include a word of rebuke and a call to repentance, even that would come over as *paraklēsis* (lit. 'calling alongside', 'encouragement'). Prophecy presented itself, where it was genuine, not as down-talking from one who claimed to be on a higher plane of spiritual reality, but as an insight into where the church or its leaders were in relation to the purposes of God.

2. 'Prophecy ... is for believers' (1 Cor. 14:22)

This does not imply that prophecy could not be meaningful to any unbelievers who were present, as we shall see later in our discussion. But it does suggest that the form of prophecy distinguished it from teaching or preaching, which might have involved a direct invitation to unbelievers to come to faith in Christ. Prophecy was addressed to the church as a sign of God's presence to make real his promises. But God's signs have two sides. One side points to the blessing promised to faith; the other to the danger of unbelief.

3. 'When you come together, everyone has a ... revelation' (1 Cor. 14:26)

While this may imply criticism of the disorderly state of worship (emphasizing 'everyone'), it is likely that Paul wanted to encourage full participation in worship within the guidelines he laid down. Prophecy ('revelation') was offered along with praise, teaching and interpreted tongues (although there is a sense in which Paul was barely tolerating the use of tongues at all in public worship – in 1 Cor. 14:4, 18–19 he seems to imply that tongues are best suited to private devotions, and uninterpreted tongues are banned entirely in 1 Cor. 14:28).

As we have noted, Paul's description of 'revelation' does not imply a form of prophecy in which a message was presented as the very words of God. What made such insights revelation was that (in the estimation of the prophet) they were the result of

119

the prompting of the Holy Spirit and were offered to the church assembled in worship or to church leaders met to make decisions. What they revealed did not claim to be on a par with Scripture, nor did prophecies appear to offer a form of divine guidance which would become obsolete after the completion of the apostolic writings. Christian prophets might offer insights into teaching already received, into what God was saying to the church and the world through historical events, or into the development of a deeper relationship with God (see pp. 87–92). The 'unveiling' involved was never comparable with the revealing of truth by those who were channels of the word (*logos*) of God. Nor was it equivalent to the exposition of that truth through the teaching ministry.

So much for the *form* of Christian prophecy in 1 Corinthians in particular. What of the *content*? What sort of things did prophets speak about? We have noted in passing that Christian prophets did not claim to offer new truths to add to the *logos*, the message of God revealed in Christ. They did not think of their prophecies as messages which demanded absolute obedience. They offered insights which they believed had been revealed to them by God. Those who heard what they said would receive such prophecies with respect, weighing what was said as one might do in response to the application of a sermon or to counsel given by a pastor. They would consider it in the light of its compatibility with scriptual teaching (which when 1 Corinthians was written was largely based on the Old Testament Scriptures) and the apostolic doctrine which was available by circulation of letters or oral tradition. Doubtless they would also test prophecy against their own experience of what they knew to be right and true.

As we have seen, there is evidence that the content of Christian prophecy might include *prediction* of the future (Acts 11:27–30; 21:11). It might also contain *insights into the human condition*, exposing the underlying thoughts and sins of people so that they are better prepared to face the judgment of God and more aware of the reality of God in their daily experience (1 Cor. 14:24–25, *cf.* Rom. 2:16). Prophecy might focus upon those whom God was calling to exercise specific ministries in the church, as in the case of Timothy, who was reminded by Paul that his call to preach and teach was confirmed by prophetic utterance (1 Tim. 1:18; 4:14). We might call this *guidance for important decisions*, whether for individuals or church leaders who are meeting to seek God's will.

While it is tempting to try to read between the lines of the New Testament for morsels of prophetic content, we will leave such speculation to those better qualified to engage in critical analysis.[1] But if we are correct in suggesting that as revelation prophecy might refer to the clarification of teaching already received (*cf.* Phil. 3:15), we can imagine that prophets might well have offered insights which helped to apply the teaching of Jesus and his apostles to the situation in which the early church actually lived and worked.

We need, however, to distinguish between

---

[1]Aune, *Prophecy in Early Christianity*, pp. 233–245, rejects the thesis of many scholars that Christian prophecy was a source of many of the sayings of Jesus which are recorded in the Gospels, and that they were originally uttered in the name of Jesus the exalted Lord.

Christian prophecy which was based on a revelation and shared with the church or its leaders and that which might simply be described as the suitable application of preaching. Let me cite a more contemporary example, with three variants.

A young preacher arrives in a Canadian logging town to begin his ministry, and in the first few weeks discovers that many people in his congregation are involved in the pilfering of wood from their employers. Shortly after this discovery, he feels compelled to preach on the text 'You shall not steal', and expounds the biblical teaching with general application. At the church door, however, his congregation congratulates him on his fine sermon, without seeming to accept that it applies directly to themselves. The following Sunday he reannounces his text as 'You shall not steal *logs*'. The reaction is somewhat different!

In this instance, while the young man may have suffered in a way similar to Jeremiah, we cannot classify what he said as Christian prophecy as described in 1 Corinthians 14. What he said did not depend on a revelation, an insight into matters which could not be gleaned purely from scriptural knowledge. He became aware of the situation either by observation or by eye-witness testimony, and saw the application of clear biblical teaching to the problem. Had he preached on stealing logs without receiving such information, we might well have suspected that he was speaking on the basis of a revelation and thought of his preaching as prophetic.

But what if, to change the scenario, that young man decides to hang fire on his message? Here he knows that sooner or later he will have to deal with the subject, it is a problem which cannot be ignored. But he is concerned to get to know his people before launching into controversy. What if he prays that God would show him the right time to speak about the issue, and, some time later, during the course of a sermon, feels compelled by the Spirit to share what God has shown him – not merely that stealing logs is wrong, but that, in ways that he can cite from his experience of the people, the life of that church and community is being sapped by their toleration of evil among them? He shares an insight which clearly exposes the reality of the situation and brings God's direction to the church. It is not just a matter of the need of repentance and the restoring of a broken trust; the preacher feels compelled to say that the leading elder, who is involved in the pilfering, should go to the manager of the logging company and apologize on behalf of all his fellow Christians for allowing the practice to continue without any questions being asked. What if the people are struck by a real sense of penitence, and the next day an elders' meeting is called to discuss the preacher's suggestion, with the result that the action is taken as he had suggested? Would we not think of that as a clear case of Christian prophecy in the Pauline tradition?

Or, to think of a slightly different scenario, let us imagine that the young preacher has, after that initial preaching of the principles involved in the commandment, decided to say nothing further from the pulpit, praying that God would convict his people in his own time. Then in an elders' meeting the matter is raised by one of the elders, who reminds the others of what the preacher has said, and how breaking God's commandments is not just wrong but harmful. He cites examples of his experience of church and community to show that the corrupt practice in question has led to many other questionable activities. He says that he feels God is saying to the church that it must put its own house in order if the gospel is to be heard in the community. Now is the time to take action; unless they do so, the church will continue to decline and the young people of the town will continue to be alienated from it.

If the worship service had been ordered in such a way that discussion could take place after the sermon it might have been possible for that elder to have shared his concern earlier. When the time came, however, he felt compelled to share his word of prophecy. What he said in fact contained all three of the elements which we have discerned as being valid content of Christian prophecy. There was a prediction that unless they repented God's judgment would fall on them; there were specific insights into the sin and its effects; and there was a call to the leaders of the church to make an important decision which would affect the direction they were taking. Yet it was offered humbly by a man who was not claiming to be blameless and who was not expecting to be received as if he were Jeremiah himself declaring the word of the Lord. He spoke with conviction yet he believed that the Holy Spirit would guide in the discussion which ensued.

I have spent time on this extended illustration to help us to see that the form and content of Christian prophecy as described by Paul is something that we may well have experienced in the life of the church, although not calling it prophecy as such.

Many have experienced that prophetic word from the pulpit, in an elders' meeting or in a house group, and have been convinced that God was really there, making his presence, and his point, felt. Few, however, may have considered that kind of thing to be prophecy.

Study of the form and content of prophecy as experienced in the Corinthian church shows that we perhaps need to reassess our concept of prophecy. Even if we have not thought of prophecy as an ecstatic experience as such, we have often tended to remove it from the ordinary and practical affairs of our churches and imagine that prophecy, if it exists, must address only high-flown themes and be the exclusive concern of respected national and international figures who may from time to time declare what they feel God is saying to the churches and the world. Not so, according to 1 Corinthians. In fact we must conclude this chapter by looking more closely at the *function* of Christian prophecy as described by Paul in that letter.

The function of Christian prophecy

If we are to test claims to prophecy in today's church, we must be sure of what was understood to be the function of Christian prophecy in the early church. What was distinctive about such prophecy? What did it achieve that would not have been accomplished by other word-ministries, such as teaching or exhortation?

While Paul says that prophecy brings strengthening, encouragement, and comfort (1 Cor. 14:3) to the assembled church, we have noted that in other places Paul speaks of preaching/teaching in similar terms (*cf.* 2 Tim. 4:2). He was keen to encourage intelligible ministry so that the church could be instructed (1 Cor. 14:19), and refers to prophecy and preaching as being involved in the process of instruction ('For you can all prophesy in turn so that everyone may be instructed and encouraged,' 1 Cor. 14:31; 'When you come together, everyone has a hymn, or a word of instruction, a revelation . . .', 1 Cor. 14:26).

All of the spiritual gifts which contributed to the worship at Corinth were to be used for the strengthening of the church (1 Cor. 14:26), so what was distinctive about the instruction which prophecy brought to the believers? In what way in particular was the church strengthened by prophecy?

Prophecy of this type functioned primarily as a *sign* of the presence of God in the midst of his church (1 Cor. 14:22–25). As we have noted in passing, God's signs are always double-sided. One side points to the blessing promised to faith; the other side warns of the danger of unbelief. So the same event or phenomenon could be said to be a sign both to believers and unbelievers. The supreme sign is of course Jesus Christ himself, and in John's Gospel the miracles of our Lord are spoken of as 'signs' which point to Jesus as the Son of God and reveal his glory (Jn. 2:11). John understood the significance of the coming of Christ as pointing believers to eternal life and pronouncing judgment on those who rejected the Son (Jn. 3:36).

We are not surprised to find that prophecy is spoken of as a sign in 1 Corinthians 14:22: 'prophecy . . . is [a sign] for believers, not for unbelievers'. Yet later in the same section Paul

126

describes the effect of prophecy in the church as convincing visiting unbelievers of the presence of God among them (1 Cor. 14:25). This seems to imply that the primary purpose of prophecy is not evangelistic, but to encourage believers. Prophecy brings insights into God's attitude to the church; his assurance that he is really with them, or his rebuke and warning; his praise or blame; his leading or obstruction. It confirms the presence of God in a remarkable way, for the church is encouraged to live out the truths which have been taught in the particular age and geographical location in which it lives.

Through prophecy of this kind, the church at Corinth was enabled to cope with the many problems they faced in applying the gospel to a complex, multicultural situation. God would show them the areas of concern which should be dealt with at any particular time. He would lead them to plan a strategy which would reach that vast seaport for Christ, and to find the leaders to implement it. Through prophecy the church might be directed to parts of Scripture which would open up their understanding of God's will. For example, when Christians were faced with intransigent opposition, a prophet might recall the response of Nehemiah (Ne. 4:1–23; 6:1–19), and feel compelled to suggest to the church that it was time they studied his message in depth. It would have been the teacher's job to expound the word of God contained therein if it was agreed that this was a timely suggestion. Yet if left to the preacher the church might still be dealing with another part of the *logos* which was not necessarily as relevant at the time.

127

Every preacher would surely pray for that prophetic sensitivity to be sure that what he was addressing did not amount to tilting at windmills! Martin Luther once berated preachers of his own day for failing to speak to the real issues of the time, suggesting that if they did not address the areas which were then under the attack of the devil, they were failing in their duty.

A church which is being taught a message which is applied in a living way, with prophetic insight into God's attitude towards his people in their particular situation, is an impressive church. It makes an impact on those who seek God, as Paul says:

> But if an unbeliever or someone who does not understand comes in while everybody is prophesying, he will be convinced by all that he is a sinner and will be judged by all, and the secrets of his heart will be laid bare. So he will fall down and worship God, exclaiming, 'God is really among you!' (1 Cor. 14:24–25).

But this can hardly mean that everybody is actually taking part in offering prophetic words – a situation which Paul has clearly discouraged. He may be focusing on 'everybody' and speaking of the impact created by different kinds of people prophesying together. Or it might be a way of describing the involvement of the whole congregation in the discussion which was initiated by the insights shared by prophets.

This assumes that prophecy functioned through a discussion in which a number of people took part (which Paul restricted to two or three, 1 Cor. 14:29), and which the whole church was able to listen to so that all might weigh carefully what was said (1 Cor. 14:29). The purpose was to instruct and encourage the whole church (1 Cor. 14:31), but there was an evangelistic by-product. When the church is functioning as the church should, that is good news! This is an important point.

We have ruled out one common misunderstanding regarding the way God operated in the church, showing that the 'word of knowledge' is not, in the New Testament, something like extrasensory perception by which leaders of meetings can have amazing insights into the problems and needs of people in the congregation. That does not mean, however, that we rule out the possibility that God may speak to people in a very personal way in a worship service. Paul clearly expected prophecy to have a very direct effect on the consciences of some unbelievers who were present in the church at Corinth at any given time. If the secrets of a person's heart could be laid bare, then it was possible that a word of prophecy might contain personal details which could have been made known only by revelation. There is no evidence, however, that this kind of thing was to be practised in a premeditated way. The conviction of sin and the sense of being exposed to the judgment of God of which Paul speaks here need not be thought of as the result of some form of telepathy which was exercised in any premeditated way. It is surely part of the work of the Holy Spirit promised by Jesus when he said: 'When he comes, he will convict the world of guilt in regard to sin and righteousness and judgment' (Jn. 16:8). It is an aspect of spiritual experience which David shared in when he reflected: 'Where can I go from your Spirit . . . Search

129

me, O God, and know my heart; test me and know my anxious thoughts. See if there is any offensive way in me, and lead me in the way everlasting' (Ps. 139:7a, 23–24; *cf.* Heb. 4:12–13).

When the church as 'the body of Christ' actually functions as a body, with all the parts working harmoniously together, there is a great witness to the reality of God. Included in that witness, in Paul's estimation, is the gift of prophecy, and when that gift functions properly and in an orderly fashion God is able to make his presence felt in a remarkable way, so that enquirers may feel that he is there and that they cannot hide from him. Prophecy is a powerful sign of God's attitude towards both believers and unbelievers, to encourage faith and to warn against unbelief.

To summarize: the function of prophecy as a sign of God's reality was seen in three areas in Paul's teaching. (They are not listed in order of priority.)

First, it functioned as an evangelistic tool whereby unbelievers visiting the church might come under conviction of sin and become aware of God's presence with his people. Secondly, we may assume that if the Spirit could touch unbelievers through prophecy then he might also convict Christians of their sin and call them to renewed repentance. Thirdly, prophecy served to confirm God's blessing on a church, that he was really with his people and would cause the fellowship to grow. In some cases prophecy might have the obverse effect, confirming God's judgment on a wayward fellowship and summoning the church to repent.[1]

In this chapter we have considered the form,

[1]W. Grudem, *The Gift of Prophecy in 1 Corinthians* (Washington, DC: University Press of America, 1982), pp. 181–207.

content and function of Christian prophecy as described in the New Testament. We must now ask, Who was entitled to prophesy? Was it restricted to a definite class of persons who were set apart for that purpose? Who were called 'prophets' in the New Testament church? And why does Paul seem to contradict himself when on the one hand he speaks of women who prophesy (1 Cor. 11:5) and yet urges women to keep silent in the churches (1 Cor. 14:34)?

For further thought and discussion

1. Why is it so important to distinguish between prophecy which claimed an absolute verbal authority and other prophetic phenomena in the New Testament?
2. What was different about the way in which Christian prophets offered their insights to the church, as distinct from the pronouncements of the apostles?
3. Do you feel threatened by the fact that Agabus got some of his details wrong?
4. Think of situations in the life of your church today in which you can see the need for Christian prophecy which might lead your fellowship into the future, realistically facing up to human weakness yet believing that God can clearly guide his people through important decisions. Pray that God would grant prophetic insights to your leaders and others.
5. If worship and decision-making meetings were not separate in our church diaries, would prophecy become more real in our experience?

8/Anyone for prophecy?

Arnold Bittlinger has helpfully distinguished between gifts and ministries in the New Testament church.[1] According to Paul, spiritual gifts (*charismata*) are not, primarily, settled abilities to exercise specific functions but instance the gracious work of the Holy Spirit through believers. In 1 Corinthians 12:4–6 Paul says: 'There are different kinds of *gifts*, but the same Spirit. There are different kinds of *service*, but the same Lord. There are different kinds of *working*, but the same God works all of them in all men.' Every time a believer is given a message of wisdom or knowledge, the power to heal or to prophesy, the grace (*charis*) of God is at work, giving a spiritual gift (*charisma*) to his church, 'the manifestation of the Spirit ... for the common good' (1 Cor. 12:7).

But Paul also indicates that God has appointed some members of the body of Christ to exercise regular ministry, to be regular channels of the various gifts. Nobody is used to exercise all the gifts, as Paul teaches in 1 Corinthians 12:27–30, but every believer is to desire to be used by the Spirit and is especially to covet 'the greater gifts'

---

[1]A. Bittlinger, *Gifts and Graces* (London: Hodder & Stoughton, 1967); *Gifts and Ministries* (London: Hodder and Stoughton, 1974).

(1 Cor. 12:31), particularly the gift of prophecy (1 Cor. 14:1).

'Office' or 'function'?

It has been forcibly argued by Wayne Grudem that there was probably no 'office' of prophet within the New Testament church.[1] But this assertion is somewhat misleading. By 'office' we mean an official recognition of special ministry. For example, there is clear evidence that some in the early church were set apart as overseers or elders, who led the church through preaching and pastoral care, and as deacons, who majored on the practical service which the churches offered to the needy in their care, including widows and orphans (*cf.* 1 Tim. 3:1–13). So Paul could include 'overseers and deacons' in his opening greetings to the church at Philippi (Phil. 1:1) because everybody would know who they were. They were not people who exercised those functions on a casual basis, they had been officially recognized. From what we know of the church of Corinth this does not appear to have been the case with prophets. Probably everybody in the Corinthian church would have known who the overseers and deacons were, but when Paul refers to prophets he says: 'If anybody *thinks he is a prophet* or spiritually gifted . . . (1 Cor. 14:37).

In 1 Corinthians 14:26–40 Paul is challenging those who were disrupting the fellowship by practising prophecy in a disorderly way. At the very least they were casting some doubts on Paul's authority or failing to bring their prophecies

[1] W. Grudem, *The Gift of Prophecy in 1 Corinthians* (Washington, DC: University Press of America, 1982), pp. 231–234, 256–257.

under the overall authority of God's word. Paul's remarks are pretty sarcastic: 'So you think you're a prophet! Then let me tell you this . . .'! It would be unwise to suggest that Paul is encouraging subjective evaluation on the part of prophets rather than acknowledging a recognized function. It is true that we would not in normal circumstances say 'If anyone *thinks* he is an elder . . .' (We can soon check up on that; and Paul would have been able to as well, as they were ordained by the laying on of hands [1 Tim. 5:22] and others could testify to their ordination.) But we may use the words sarcastically, 'So you think you're an *elder*!' – not because we are doubting a person's credentials, but because we are challenging whether he is worthy of such a title or is exercising his office properly. It is a mistake to place too much weight on 1 Corinthians 14:37 in view of the implicit sarcasm in Paul's remarks here. Remember that he has just fired this salvo: 'Did the word of God originate with you? Or are you the only people it has reached?' (1 Cor. 14:36). If that isn't sarcastic, what is?

Besides, we do have evidence from Acts that some were recognized as prophets, even if they were never set apart in a similar way to elders or deacons. Agabus (Acts 21:10, *etc.*), Judas and Silas (Acts 15:32) are referred to as 'prophets'. The latter pair were never sent to the church at Antioch at one time with an important letter from Jerusalem, and we are told that after the reading of the apostolic letter they said much to encourage and strengthen the brothers. Then they returned to Jerusalem. They clearly did not just 'think of themselves' as prophets. Others recognized that God had raised them up to exercise an important ministry, whatever

134

their self-awareness may have been. While Paul and Barnabas taught and preached the word of God in Antioch (Acts 15:35), Judas and Silas encouraged and strengthened the believers in a matter which involved specific direction about an issue which was troubling the church, that of how the Gentile believers should respond to Judaistic pressures for them to observe Jewish food laws. Their prophecy encouraged the church to do the right thing in the specific situation of the day. Prophets like these two men must have been regarded highly to have been appointed delegates of the apostles. Like Barnabas, they were encouragers who mobilized the church for active obedience to God's directions.

In the New Testament church there were recognized prophets who were consulted when important decisions had to be made. And yet, as we noted in the case of Agabus' advice to Paul, they were not considered infallible. So in Corinth there were also prophets in the church, appointed (lit. 'placed') by God as Paul had been appointed as an apostle (1 Cor. 12:28), and recognized by the whole church. It was because they were prophets that the others (the rest of the congregation) would listen carefully to the discussion which took place among them (1 Cor. 14:29) and weigh carefully what was said. Those who exercised the prophetic ministry could learn to be sensitive to the other prophets so that they could all contribute in turn (1 Cor. 14:31).

In contrast to this view Wayne Grudem suggests that anyone was eligible to prophesy in the Corinthian church gathering and that all who prophesied were termed 'prophets'. That is, anyone who received a revelation and waited his or her turn could share it in the proper part of the worship meeting. This was subject to guidelines as to how many should take part, so that all would be done in an orderly way.

It is certainly true that all of the believers were encouraged to seek to prophesy (1 Cor. 14:1, 39). The potential was there for all to prophesy, but not all would be given the gift (1 Cor. 12:29). 'You can all prophesy *one by one*' (1 Cor. 14:31, author's translation) certainly does not mean that all could actually prophesy. The emphasis is on 'one-by-one'. In other words those who prophesied were not out of control and chaos did not need to result if prophecy was encouraged. No prophet could conjure up a revelation, however, but had to wait until some matter was unveiled to him or her.

Spontaneity was the characteristic of this prophetic discussion, with each participant encouraged to stand up to make a point, presumably so that the whole gathering might hear and so be instructed and encouraged (1 Cor. 14:31). As we have noted, however, this does not necessarily mean that the revelation shared with the church was a completely new flash of insight. It might be that the prophet felt that God had impressed on his or her consciousness an awareness that the right time had come to contribute a matter which had been chewed over for some time.

Grudem's functional definition of 'prophet', that anybody who prophesied could be called by that title, does not seem to fit the evidence in 1 Corinthians 12 – 14 and Ephesians. We would doubtless be mistaken to think that Paul 'ordained' people to office as prophets, miracle-workers, healers, administrators, *etc.* (1 Cor. 12:23–30). Clearly such charismatic service would have been initially recognized as being of God and showing potential for further ministry, but that does not mean that they held any office other than that of overseer or deacon. Prophecy is so important in Paul's estimation, however, that we cannnot imagine that he was not concerned to delimit prophets in any way. True, he encouraged all believers in Corinth to seek to prophesy, to correct their over-emphasis on tongues (1 Cor. 14:1–5). He does speak of a scenario where 'everybody is *prophesying*' (1 Cor. 14:24), but this can hardly mean that everybody is actually taking part in offering prophetic words – a situation which Paul has clearly discouraged. He may be focusing on 'everybody' and speaking of the impact created by different kinds of people prophesying together. Or it might be a way of describing the involvement of the whole congregation in the discussion which was instigated by the insights shared by prophets.

Paul's use of the word 'prophets' is very limited (1 Cor. 12:28–29; 14:29,32; Eph. 2:20; 3:5; 4:11). In every case except the 1 Corinthians 14 references it is clear that Paul used 'prophets' to describe a distinct and important group. In Ephesians 2:20 and 3:5 we have argued that Paul is not separating apostles and prophets but is referring to the 'apostles-who-are-also-prophets' (see pp. 74–81). But this would have been meaningless if 'prophet' could have been applied to anybody who ever prophesied. It is significant, however, that Paul should class himself as both an apostle and a Christian prophet if there was among his hearers an awareness of the important ministry exercised by those who were prophets but not apostles.

Paul uses the verb 'to prophesy' in a much wider way, as describing an activity which involved, on an occasional basis, a much larger number of believers. Men or women (1 Cor. 11:5) might prophesy within certain guidelines concerning attitude and good order, and in proportion to a person's faith (Rom. 12:6). A large number might be involved in prophesying at any one time (1 Cor. 14:24), yet not all were 'prophets'.

A tentative solution

Here I offer to this problem a possible solution which seems to do justice to the evidence. First, we must take into account that some were recognized as prophets not simply because they had pro-phesied on occasion but because they had been appointed by God (1 Cor. 12:28), even if the church did not ordain them in any official way. Others would be able to recognize that God had given such prophets a prophetic ministry, and prophets (*e.g.* Judas and Silas, as we noted earlier) might even travel to other congregations. Church leaders such as overseers and deacons would be on the look-out for those (including prophets) whom God was calling to specific ministries. We know from early church history that prophets continued to function at the end of the first century AD, and probably for much longer.[1]

Secondly, the possibility of recognizing new 'prophets' suggests that it must have been possible

[1] F. F. Bruce, *The Spreading Flame* (Exeter: Paternoster Press, 1958), pp. 92, 214–220.

for believers to offer a word of prophecy, even if they did not do so again. Only in that way could someone begin to share in prophecy and be recognized by the church. Surely that could well have taken place during the 'weighing' of prophecies which Paul describes (1 Cor. 14:29), in which the whole congregation was involved in thoughtful assessment of what prophets said, and during which the men could actually express opinions as to the value or otherwise of the prophecies, depending on their conformity to Scripture and other teaching received from the apostles by word of mouth.

A paraphrase of 1 Corinthians 14:29–35 may help to clarify the possible scenario:

> At the most, two or three prophets already recognized as exercising a prophetic ministry should speak following the word of teaching. To make sure everybody can hear, those who prophesy should stand up in turn. If one prophet feels that he or she can't hold back a contribution any longer, however, let the speaker give way to let him or her have his or her say. Yet prophets should remember that they can easily prophesy one by one, and there is no need for the discussion to get out of control. The Spirit who prompts them to prophesy brings peace to the church wherever he is truly manifested, and true Christian prophets are well able to participate in such a way that two or three who are recognized as prophets can participate helpfully. The prophetic discussion should be carefully considered by the whole congregation, who should seek the

139

Spirit's help to discern what is valuable in the prophecies and what is not. The meeting will then be open for further discussion, and all men will be eligible to take part. Women, however, should offer their opinions at home and discuss them with their husbands, to avoid any temptation to ask critical questions, or to offer teaching. Husbands of spiritual discernment will be able to encourage their wives to prophesy in church when it is appropriate.

In reading the passage this way we have preserved the place of the recognized prophet, yet have also accepted that others might contribute to the discussion in such a way that potential prophets might be noticed (and because prophecy was subject to the granting of revelations there was no need for that kind of liberty to become a liability!).

Prophecy and the silence of women

This interpretation does, however, involve certain conclusions about the role of women in the church. That women could contribute a word of prophecy is clear from 1 Corinthians 11:5, where Paul speaks of the attitude expected of women who pray or prophesy in worship. They are to recognize the leadership of their husbands and submit to their authority. Nobody can disagree that there are cases of female prophets in the New Testament, although Philip's daughters (Acts 21:9) are described as 'four unmarried daughters *who prophesied*', and not as prophetesses. Yet when we come to 1 Corinthians 14:34 we meet with difficulty, as Paul says that women should *remain silent* in the churches. If this was a complete ban on female contributions to worship services it would contradict 1 Corinthians 11:5 and make a nonsense of Paul's teaching in the rest of 1 Corinthians 14, where there is no indication that his encouragement of prophecy was limited to men only.

The problem is not as great as it may seem. The Greek verb 'to keep silent' (*sigaō*) seldom if ever refers to a total ban on any form of speech. The silence is always qualified by a restriction defined by the context. It might be a time restriction, to keep silent while another is speaking, as in 1 Corinthians 14:30, where a prophet is to be silent in order to let another speak, not to shut up for the rest of the meeting! Silence might also be appropriate with reference to certain topics, but not in other cases. Paul commands tongues-speakers to be silent in the church worship if there was no interpreter, but that did not ban their participation in other ways.

What then is the contextual restriction in the particular section where Paul says:

> As in all the congregations of the saints, women should remain silent in the churches. They are not allowed to speak, but must be in submission, as the law says. If they want to inquire about something, they should ask their own husbands at home; for it is disgraceful for a woman to speak in the church (1 Cor. 14:33b–35).

After detailed analysis, Grudem suggests[1] that it refers to silence during the weighing of prophecies, when the whole congregation would consider carefully and test to see whether prophecies

[1]Grudem, *Gift of Prophecy in 1 Corinthians*, pp. 251–255.

were truly from God in all that they contained. This is consistent with the use of the verbs 'keep silent' and 'speak' in the New Testament, and with Paul's teaching on the submission of women. Women who criticized a prophecy, expressing their opinion regarding whether it was really a reflection of God's will for the church, would be assuming a role which Paul would not have encouraged. He clearly believed that women should be subordinate to men and not exercise authority through a teaching ministry (1 Tim. 2:12–15). That is why Paul indicates that women should ask questions of their husbands at home. As experience of church meetings shows, even questions can be worded as criticisms! While it is possible to derive a principle of subordination in authority from certain Old Testament passages, as Paul does, it is quite impossible to derive a general principle of silence for women in worship in the same way.[1]

To summarize: Paul encouraged all to seek the gift of prophecy. While believers are right to ask for spiritual gifts, such gifts are sovereignly granted by God the Spirit. As Jesus taught, 'How much more will your Father in heaven give the the Holy Spirit to those who ask him!' (Lk. 11:13b). Yet Paul also recognized that although every believer had the right to ask not all would be given what they requested. And he also expected God to raise up appointed prophets who would exercise a regular prophetic ministry in the churches and even perhaps be itinerant. In order

[1]See J. B. Hurley, *Man and Woman in Biblical Perspective* (Leicester: IVP, 1981), pp. 162–194.

for that to be recognized, however, those who prophesied had to start somewhere, and that was possible through the evaluation (in church or at home) of the prophetic input which followed the teaching of God's word.

Seeking the gift of prophecy

How does Paul suggest believers should seek the gift of prophecy? First, by praying for the gift (*cf*. 1 Cor. 14:13); second, by being content with their present gifts (1 Cor. 12:18); third, by being mature (1 Cor. 14:37); fourth, by having the right motives (1 Cor. 14:1); fifth, by using their present gifts (1 Cor. 14:12,26); sixth, by learning to listen to what God is saying to their church situation (1 Cor. 14:30); seventh, by not being afraid to share, as all prophecy is open to testing (1 Cor. 14:29).

The encouragement to seek spiritual gifts that God would work in a particular way through oneself must be balanced by Paul's teaching on the sovereignty of God. The Spirit distributes his gifts to each as he wills; he is the expert manager who delegates carefully (1 Cor. 12:11) and places people with certain gifts in the church (1 Cor. 12:28). Yet Christians are not to be passive about their part within the body of Christ. They are encouraged to ask the manager for more responsibility as they grow in faith. When Jesus taught his disciples to ask for the Holy Spirit (Lk. 11:13), he related that to a father's desire to give good gifts to his children. Because of this, Paul had no hesitation in exhorting the Corinthians to ask God for those spiritual gifts which would be of greatest use, especially prophecy (1 Cor. 12:31; 14:1,39).

This implies that prayer is essential. We cannot receive unless we ask. Yet neither pride (1 Cor. 12:20–24) nor jealousy (1 Cor. 12:14–19) should be our motivation for asking. Nor should believers be complaining and discontented with what they have already been given to share. If prophecy is linked with spiritual maturity (1 Cor. 14:37), then it may well be that, as with wisdom and understanding (1 Cor. 2:6,14), prophecy is more often granted to those who are mature in faith. In fact the exhortation to seek prophecy may be another way of encouraging maturity. A sure sign of Christian maturity is that growing insight into the way God is guiding his people at any given time.

The right motivation is of course love – the unselfish desire to be a means of building up the church (1 Cor. 14:1, 12). In this way self-aggrandizement is exposed as an unworthy motive. A sign of love is that Christians are seeking to do to the best of their ability the work which they have already been given. God gives more to those who have proven faithful with lesser tasks (Mt. 25:21).

To learn to listen for God's directions to his church today is the key to the exercising of the prophetic gift. Doubtless Paul linked this with attentiveness to the teaching of God's word and earnest prayer in fellowship with others. God can plant insights in the hearts and minds of those who seek him, and he has provided ways of evaluating the response shared. Within the pattern of our church meetings there must be time for listening as well as speaking; there must be room for response by the people as well as declarations by the preacher. This may be through a small-group structure, where people are more likely to be willing to share, or through a church prayer meeting, where those who seek God's blessing on his work are gathered in united intercession.

In encouraging all believers earnestly to seek the gift of prophecy Paul is not suggesting that prophecy should be thought of as a commonplace experience which very many believers would regularly share in. The thrust of his argument in 1 Corinthians 12 – 14 is that prophecy is precious and is to be sought because of its importance in the building up of Christ's church. By contrast Paul seems to indicate that tongues may well have been experienced by many more in the Corinthian church and that there was a tendency to over-emphasize its importance in Christian corporate worship. Paul spoke in tongues, but he preferred to use tongues in private devotions (1 Cor. 14:4, 18–19) rather than in public worship. His instructions were geared to remove the babble of uninter-preted tongues so that there would be more room for intelligible words (including prophecy) which might instruct others (1 Cor. 14:19). But that does not suggest that the babble of tongues was to be replaced by a plethora of prophets! To use an image from television, perhaps the prophets were like the panel in *Question Time* and the rest of the congregation were like the audience (and permit-ted to express their evaluation of the panel's con-tributions in a limited way).

We often encourage people to seek something, not because it is easily obtained, but because it is valuable. It seems that Paul encouraged the Cor-inthians to seek to prophesy because, although any believer might be used by the Holy Spirit to bring a

145

timely insight to God's people, it would be a special experience in most believer's lives and few would be called to exercise a prophetic ministry as such. The fact that very few are termed prophets in the New Testament church suggests that it was an outstanding ministry.

Anyone for prophecy? In theory, yes: any believer could rightly ask God for the gift of prophecy. In practice, no: prophecy is a precious manifestation of the Spirit which must be sought with great determination. It might be received only occasionally or even but once. In some cases a prophetic ministry might be established where a 'prophet' was raised up by God and 'placed' within the church(es).

But is this conclusion purely academic? Is this prophetic gift still available today? In chapter 9 we must ask whether New Testament prophecy in all its forms has ceased to be operative.

For further thought and discussion

1. Why are spiritual gifts spoken of as works of service (1 Cor. 12:4–6)?
2. Think of ways in which you might discern that God was using a fellow Christian to bring prophetic insights. How would you react if somebody suggested that you showed prophetic tendencies?
3. If Paul encouraged believers to seek to prophesy, was it because it was very rare or because it was freely available to all?
4. Look at the seven ways in which Paul encouraged Christians to seek the gift of prophecy in 1 Corinthians 14:13, *etc*. (See p. 143). Study each

verse in turn and pray over the teaching.
5. Have you ever asked God for the gift of prophecy? Discuss this with others.

9/Has prophecy ceased?

In chapter 1 I referred to a survey which I carried out as part of my research for this book. One of the questions put to the church leaders in the survey concerned whether they thought prophecy was a thing of the past. In response to the question, 'Is prophecy a spiritual gift which God no longer gives to his church?' seventy-four per cent of the sample said 'No'. This is an interesting response from those within the Reformed tradition, which has often classified prophecy as one of the 'signs of the apostles' (cf. 2 Cor. 12:12) and therefore a special miraculous provision which God granted to the apostolic church to confirm the truth of the message proclaimed by Christ's ambassadors. When the canon of Scripture was completed, it is argued, the need for the gift of prophecy disappeared for one of two reasons. First, if prophecy was a special gift which God granted for the guidance of the church it would have become obsolete when Scripture was fully available because the Holy Spirit could apply its teaching and supply all the guidance required. Secondly, if prophecy was one aspect of the revelation of the word of God in New Testament times, some of which was included in the prophetic writings we call the New Testament, then clearly there was no further need for prophecy once the canon was closed.

The case for cessation

The *cessation of charismata* was propounded forcefully by Benjamin B. Warfield a hundred years ago[1] and still holds sway in much Reformed thinking. A recent exponent of the position is Richard B. Gaffin, and we must consider the validity of his particular case for cessation.[2]

What Gaffin says about Christian prophecy is based on certain assumptions which must be questioned. His most crucial presupposition is that as a whole prophecy at Corinth was the same phenomenon as that which is described in the Pauline writings elsewhere, in Acts and in Revelation. In making this assumption Gaffin does not consider the possibility that there may have been different kinds of prophecy in the New Testament. Because of this he concludes that prophecy as a revelatory gift always brings to the church the words of God in the primary and original sense: 'Prophecy is not, at least primarily or as one of its necessary marks, the interpretation of an already existing inspired text or oral tradition but is itself the inspired, nonderivative word of God.'[3]

To support this thesis Gaffin reminds us of the fact that Paul speaks of Christian prophecy as 'revelation'. But he does not consider the possibility that this might be a reference to the idea of revelation which we have noted in Philippians 3:15 and Ephesians 1:17. In chapter 6 we dealt with this

[1] B. B. Warfield, *Counterfeit Miracles* (reissue Edinburgh: Banner of Truth, 1972).
[2] R. B. Gaffin, *Perspectives on Pentecost* (Grand Rapids: Baker Book House, 1979), pp. 55–116.
[3] *Ibid.*, p. 59.

at length, concluding that revelation need not always imply absolute verbal authority, and suggesting that the contextual use of the word 'revelation' is crucial. Because Paul speaks of Christian prophecy as a kind of revelation which is open to testing and evaluation we concluded that it did not, despite what Gaffin states, claim to be the very words of God.

Secondly, Gaffin bases his interpretation on the fact that in 1 Corinthians 13:2 prophecy is apparently equated with 'all mysteries and all knowledge'. As 'mystery' is in Pauline usage an important word which describes the inaccessibility of the truth of God apart from revelation, Gaffin suggests that this equates prophecy with the word of God which reveals salvation in Christ. He argues that because Paul speaks of this mystery as something previously unknown and now communicated for the first time (Rom. 11:25–32; 1 Cor. 15:51–57), prophecy must always have been part of the process of revealing the very words of God by inspiration of his servants the apostles and prophets. But this is not necessarily the case. On closer examination we can see that 1 Corinthians 13:1–3 does not seem to be concerned about precise definitions, but is really saying, 'I may know everything there is to know, but if I have no love I am nothing.'[1]

Mystery in Paul certainly does refer to the secret thoughts, plans and dispensations of God which are hidden from human reason and must be revealed (unveiled) to those for whom they are

---

[1]C. K. Barrett, *A Commentary on the First Epistle to the Corinthians* (London: A. & C. Black, [2]1971), p. 301.

intended.[1] But we have already demonstrated that as a type of revelation Christian prophecy never claimed to be the very word of God on a par with that which was recorded in Scripture, and that it might even contain elements of inaccuracy (as in the case of Agabus in Acts 21). If we insist that 1 Corinthians 13:2 is saying 'Prophecy = mysteries + knowledge', then we make Paul say something which is inconsistent with his teaching on prophecy in 1 Corinthians 14, where Christian prophecy is viewed as a phenomenon which must be evaluated for that which is truly from God. As we have seen, Paul would certainly not have encouraged believers to *weigh* his apostolic teaching in the same way (1 Cor. 14:29).

The meaning of the Greek word *diakrinō* elsewhere in 1 Corinthians is 'to distinguish' (1 Cor. 4:7) and 'to evaluate' (1 Cor. 11:31). The 'weighing' of prophecies is therefore a process in which every believer gathered for worship may listen carefully to and evaluate what prophets say, distinguishing the good from the less good, the helpful from the unhelpful, the true from the false. Paul's use of *diakrinō* in this way is a crucial part of his teaching on Christian prophecy. In the New Testament *diakrinō* is found only eighteen times, including seven times in Paul (in Romans and 1 Corinthians). In classical Greek the verb meant (a) 'to judge, make a distinction, distinguish', and it later developed the sense of (b) 'to separate, divide'. It could also describe (c) the giving of a decision or the dispensation of justice. In the

[1]W. Bauer, W. F. Arndt, F. W. Gingrich, F. W. Danker (eds), *A Greek-English Lexicon of the New Testament* (Chicago: Chicago University Press, 1979), p. 530.

Septaugint, the Greek translation of the Old Testament, the chief meaning is (a), above, but it could also mean 'to take issue' or 'to examine'.

Twice in Paul *diakrinō* means 'to judge'. In 1 Corinthians 11:31 this refers to the judgment required by individuals of themselves, in preparing to receive communion in a worthy manner. This self-examination is a testing of one's attitude and actions in relation to the sacrament, and means facing up to one's weaknesses as well as meditating on God's grace in Christ. This seems also to be the meaning of *diakrinō* in 1 Corinthians 14:29, where prophetic words are to be judged in a similar way and what is profitable (from God) distinguished from what is not (purely man-made). The idea of distinguishing in the sense of evaluation is found in 1 Corinthians 4:7, 'For who makes you different from anyone else?'

The other prominent meaning of *diakrinō* in the New Testament is 'to doubt' (eight times), often reflecting the notion that believers who doubt God are judging him falsely.

All this serves to demonstrate the fact that Paul viewed Christian prophecy as a phenomenon which required close scrutiny and was not simply to be accepted or rejected, but was to be tested for what was good, bad or indifferent (*cf.* 1 Thes. 5:19–22).[1]

Thirdly, Gaffin suggests that Ephesians 3:3–5 reinforces his argument. His interpretation is based, however, on the view that 'holy apostles and prophets' in this section refers to two distinct

[1]C. Brown (ed.), *New International Dictionary of New Testament Theology*, vol. 1 (Grand Rapids: Zondervan; Exeter: Paternoster Press, 1975), pp. 503–505.

groups. We have already sought to demonstrate that this is not necessary, and that it probably means 'apostles-who-are-also-prophets' (pp. 74–81). It is the apostles who are the only recipients of the mystery of Christ which has been made known in its fullness. That they are fundamental and unique to the Christian church is demonstrable, but that is not so with Christian prophets. The apostolic band was fixed and limited in the original sense of those commissioned by the risen Christ in a personal way. The number of Christian prophets was ever increasing in New Testament times and Paul encouraged that growth when he charged the Corinthians to be eager to prophesy (1 Cor. 14:1).

It can be seen from this introductory skirmish with Gaffin's position that all of his basic points can be understood in a different way. His understanding of Christian prophecy has been dealt with at length in virtually all that we have said so far, and I do not want to repeat myself further. The important point to note is that when Gaffin goes on to speak about the cessation of prophecy he is speaking about the cessation of the primary type of prophecy (the very word of God), which we have sought to distinguish from the secondary type (Christian prophecy). At this point it would be helpful to reaffirm that, like Gaffin, I believe that the primary type of prophecy has indeed ceased. This has been indicated in our discussion already, but it is useful to remind ourselves of the strong words at the end of the book of Revelation which seem to warn against any attempt to usurp the kind of authority which was claimed by the classical Old Testament prophets and the apostle-prophets of the New Testament and their

153

immediate associates. Absolute verbal authority died out with the apostles and is preserved in their writings (see pp. 155–157).

We have argued (pp. 74–81) that Paul considered the apostles to be the foundation-stones of the church, along with Christ the chief cornerstone (Eph. 2:20; 3:5). It was not merely their message which was foundational; their function as bearers of the absolute verbal revelation recorded in the New Testament was associated with them personally, and therefore ceased with their demise. But Gaffin does not take seriously enough the evidence for other prophetic phenomena, and his argument hardly attempts to deal with the issue. He is also confused about the gift of discernment of spirits (1 Cor. 12:10), suggesting that that gift would have had a leading part to play in the evaluation of prophecies, in a way similar to the gift of interpretation which was used to elucidate tongues-speaking in the church. This view, which has been argued in detail by the German scholar G. Dautzenberg, has been conclusively refuted by recent scholarship,[1] and it is not my intention to go into the details here. Suffice it to say that the real problem with Gaffin's position is an unwillingness to interpret prophecy in its context coupled with a tendency to imagine that 'prophecy' and its associated words must always refer to absolute verbal revelation: 'The words of the prophet are the words of God and are to be received and responded to as such.'[2]

In view of the evidence that Christian prophets

[1]W. Grudem, *The Gift of Prophecy in 1 Corinthians* (Washington, DC: University Press of America, 1982), pp. 263–288.
[2]Gaffin, *Perspectives on Pentecost*, p. 72.

were not received in such a manner – as when prophetic advice was rejected by Paul (Acts 21:4) despite the fact that Luke records that it was given 'through the Spirit' – Gaffin's confident affirmation must be challenged and rejected. If what the prophets said is to be equated with the very word of God, our understanding of verbal inspiration must come under fire. We cannot evade the distinction in Paul's mind, plainly stated in 1 Corinthians 14:37: 'If anybody thinks he is a prophet or spiritually gifted, let him acknowledge that what I am writing to you is the Lord's command.'

Prophecy, in the sense of Christian prophecy, is *not* the Lord's command. That is the characteristic of the primary type of prophecy which, as the revelation of the very word of God, we believe has ceased in accordance with Revelation 22:18–19:

> I warn everyone who hears the words of the prophecy of this book: If anyone adds anything to them, God will add to him the plagues described in this book. And if anyone takes words away from this book of prophecy, God will take away from him his share in the tree of life and in the holy city, which are described in this book.

The significance of Revelation 22:18–19

On initial encounter these stern words might seem only to apply to the book of Revelation itself, but they surely apply to all prophecy which claims an absolute verbal authority. While we might correctly assume that John's vision was closed with inspired words which were intended to signal a

155

halt to the phenomenon of verbal inspiration, and therefore defined Revelation as the last addition to the word of God, there is a broader significance in this warning. Although the subject of how the canon of Scripture was recognized and accepted is beyond our present remit, what is important for our discussion is that here we have a statement which shows clearly that we must distinguish between prophecy which claims an absolute verbal authority and the kind of Christian prophecy described in 1 Corinthians. The kind of evaluation of prophetic insights which was encouraged by Paul, in which the congregation distinguished between worthwhile and less useful contributions, is alien to the thinking of Revelation 22:18–19.

To add to or subtract from the very word of God is to rob it of its authority and to place it under the judgment of people whose powers of assessment are far from perfect. At the end of the day God's authority is usurped by man, either by subtracting unpalatable sections or by adding explanatory glosses which really impose the rationale of the interpreter on the text. The ban imposed in Revelation reflects the Mosaic guidelines of Deuteronomy 18, where presumptuous prophecy such as that was punishable by death. There is not a hint of that kind of severity in Paul's encouragement of the weighing of Christian prophecy in Corinth, while any attempt to pervert the gospel was anathema (Gal. 1:6–9).

The point is this: Revelation 22:18–19 warns against any tampering with the absolute verbal revelation contained in that prophecy. It can therefore be applied to any attempt to add to or subtract from the prophetic writings which have been received as the word of God in the Old and New Testaments. It is the last word of the last survivor of the apostolic band, John the beloved disciple, warning the churches against false prophecy which contradicted the apostolic doctrine, and indicating that verbal inspiration was unique to the apostles and their immediate associates, so that as they, like John, departed this life, the phenomenon of prophecy which claimed an absolute verbal authority would cease to be operative. Only those who had a divine commission as ambassadors for Christ (or sought like Mark or Luke to act as their spokesmen) should dare to offer prophecy of the primary type which would become part of the written word of God. The main job of the post-apostolic church was to explain and apply the received teaching, as we see in the Pastoral Epistles.

Prophecy and 'the coming of perfection'

There remains, however, one problem which we cannot avoid. We have stated our conviction that, in Paul, prophecy invariably refers to Christian prophecy. He is not in 1 Corinthians 14 encouraging believers to think of themselves as potential bearers of the words of God which might be incorporated in holy writ. He is doing what Moses did, long before, when he expressed his longing that prophetic manifestations might be given to a large number of God's people (Nu. 11:29), and following Joel's vision of a new prophetic age (Joel 2:28–29).

The problem is this: When will that new age come to its end or consummation? Is even

Christian prophecy, which God has used to guide and direct his church at least in New Testament times, a thing of the past? Has prophecy ceased, in whatever form it may have taken? This might well be our conclusion when we read in 1 Corinthians 13:8: 'Love never fails. But where there are prophecies, they will *cease* . . .' But when in Paul's estimation would that cessation take place? He goes on in verses 9–10: 'For we know in part and we prophesy in part, but *when perfection comes* the imperfect disappears.' But what is this perfection? Does it mean maturity of development, indicating that prophecy was required during the years of the church's infancy, but that now that God's people have come to manhood, as it were, it is no longer needed? Or is it possible that perfection means the completion of the canon of Scripture?

Gaffin admits that neither of these interpretations can be justified by sound exegesis. The coming of perfection is without doubt to be expected only at the parousia, the return of Christ. By comparison with the perfection to come we are all living in the age of childhood. Whatever maturity is possible for the believer in this life is a pale reflection of the perfection yet to come. 'Now we see but a poor reflection as in a mirror; then we shall see face to face' (1 Cor. 13:12). Despite this admission Gaffin will not accept that Christian prophecy would, in Paul's view, continue until the parousia. He asserts that Paul is not really addressing the issue of whether particular gifts would cease to be operative, but is speaking about the temporary and fragmentary character of present knowledge:

158

> What he does affirm is the termination of the believer's present, fragmentary knowledge, based on likewise temporary modes of revelation, when 'the perfect' comes. The time of the cessation of prophecy ... is an open question so far as this passage is concerned and will have to be decided on the basis of other passages and considerations.[1]

Surely this is theological side-stepping. Nevertheless Gaffin does confirm that some older Reformed arguments for the cessation of prophecy in all its forms are indefensible. What he fails to see, however, is that if Christian prophecy is liberated from the strait-jacket of this particular approach we may do justice to his admirable concern for the foundational nature of God's revelation in Scripture and still be able to find room for recognizing a prophetic gift. This gift is in fact so important in Paul's teaching about Christian experience that he devotes the lion's share of 1 Corinthians 12 – 14 to a detailed discussion of it. From my particular viewpoint within the Reformed perspective I find it hard to imagine that God would inspire his apostle to spend so much time on a gift which would soon become obsolete. I find it much more reasonable (at the very least) to follow the cautious approach of Calvin, who, although considering prophecy an extraordinary gift, did not rule out the possibility that God might still give it to his church at times of particular need (see pp. 20–23). Yet even that does not seem to fit with the New Testament evidence of a spiritual gift which was thought to be of such great value to the churches and their

[1]*Ibid.*, p. 111.

growth that Christians should prize it highly. Pro-phecy might be precious, but it is not in Paul's teaching part of an impossible dream!

Has prophecy ceased? The answer is twofold. Yes, both classical Old Testament prophecy and apostolic prophecy have ceased. Through that pri-mary type of prophecy God revealed his words to men and sent them out as his ambassadors, inves-ting in their message an authority which was absolute and extended to the actual words spoken and written as they communicated the *logos*, the word of God. It is my conviction, however, that there is a continuing, secondary type of prophecy, which we have termed 'Christian prophecy' and which will be given according to God's gracious will until the end of time.

The historical demise of prophecy

Before we close this chapter one further argument needs to be tackled. Church historians tell us that, although prophecy is prominent in the documents which pertain to the early days of the church's worldwide expansion, there is some evidence that it did in fact become dormant or extinct. At the beginning of the second century the prophets still occupied an honoured place in church life, although, as in the New Testament, warnings con-tinued to be made about false prophets and how to recognize them. The *Didache*, an important docu-ment of that time, speaks of prophets being involved in the celebration of the Lord's Supper (*Did.* 11–13). Yet the churches were to beware of those who traded in prophecy and asked for money. In fact they were not to listen to any such impostors. Christian prophets had to exercise exemplary behaviour, and were to be welcomed and supported by the congregation. That prophets were not operative in all congregations is clear. Many were itinerant, and their arrival in a particular fellowship should not necessarily have been a threat to the authority of elders (overseers/bishops) and deacons.[1]

Ignatius, an early bishop of Antioch in Syria, died as a martyr towards the end of the reign of Emperor Trajan (AD 98–117). On his final journey to Rome he travelled overland through Asia Minor and wrote seven letters, five of which were to local churches which he had visited *en route*. Ignatius is remembered for his belief that local bishops are earthly representatives of God or Jesus and the apostles. He referred to Christian prophets only once in his extant letters, no doubt due to his emphasis on church order and discipline, but what appear to be prophetic words have been preserved in his letters. In one famous oracle he expressed his conviction that God was using him as a prophet in order to undergird the authority of church leaders:

I cried out while I was with you,
I spoke with a great voice, with the voice of God,
'To the bishops give heed,
And to the presbytery,
And to the deacons.'

(*To the Philadelphians*, 7:1–2)

He went on to speak of certain divisive people in the church who were challenging the authority of

---

[1] D. Aune, *Prophecy in Early Christianity and the Ancient Mediterranean World* (Grand Rapids: Wm B. Eerdmans, 1983), pp. 225–226; *cf.*

161

their leaders. In exhorting the believers to love unity and to avoid divisions, Ignatius made this bold admonition: 'Apart from the bishop do nothing.' His words were received by the church at Philadelphia with a sense of wonder, because Ignatius' fleeting visit had not given him time to be aware of the situation in the church. They believed that he had prophetic insight akin to that described by Paul in 1 Corinthians 14:25, where prophecy is said to disclose the secrets of people's hearts.

F. F. Bruce makes a very astute point when reflecting on the possible area of tension between bishops like Ignatius and the itinerant prophets who had no such office within the church: 'There is, in fact, an inevitable tension between the ordered forms of regular ministry and the more unpredictable and enthusiastic forms. It frequently happens that those who appreciate one form cannot abide the other.'[1]

History records that in the year AD 95 there was a schism in the church at Corinth, as a result of such tensions, and Clement wrote from Rome to challenge the fact that some of the elders in the Corinthian church had been deposed. It seems that in response to this problem, church leaders became somewhat reactionary. They did not deal with abuses of prophecy as Paul had done; he had limited prophets' contributions to worship without stifling the prophetic word, and had positively encouraged the growth of Christian prophecy in

Grudem, *Gift of Prophecy in 1 Corinthians*, p. 291ff. As Aune observes, 'We do not hear of any prophet who accepted fees for his services and was not condemned for the practice' (p. 228).

[1]F. F. Bruce, *The Spreading Flame* (Exeter: Paternoster Press, 1958), p. 217.

the church, but they became increasingly suspicious of all prophetic claims.

With the arrival of Montanus in Asia Minor, whose story we referred to briefly in chapter 1 (p. 18), the temptation was for the Catholic church to throw the prophetic baby out with the bathwater of extremism! Yet, as Bruce notes, there must have been something of more solid worth in Montanism than is generally supposed, in view of the fact that it attracted such an able scholar as Tertullian. Some who rejected Montanism also refused to accept the canonicity of the book of Revelation, due to its popularity among Montanists! In other minds the Johannine literature as a whole became suspect.[1]

There is some considerable evidence, therefore, for suggesting that it was not for the best of reasons that Christian prophecy became an unusual phenomenon in the church and may well have been discouraged and passed into abeyance for a time. As the authority of bishops grew, without which nothing could be done or approved, the place of prophets who dared to offer insights into God's will for his church was undermined. As David Aune has suggested:

This does not mean that prophets became an endangered species primarily because of their increasing association with heretical movements, but it does suggest that the earlier role of prophets as articulators of the norms, values, and decisions of the invisible head of the

[1]*Ibid.*, p. 220; *cf.* Aune, *Prophecy in Early Christianity*, p. 313, 'All the major features of early Montanism, including the behaviour associated with possession trance, are derived from early Christianity.'

church was taken over by the visible figures of the teacher, preacher, theologian, and church leader.[1]

Much happened during those years of the growth of the power of bishops which the Reformers later challenged. In the maelstrom of the Reformation, when the centrality of Scripture was recovered by the Reformed churches, there was probably no time for reassessing attitudes to prophecy in the church. Anything which, like the received traditions of the Catholic church, might appear to have been a challenge to the authority of Scripture would surely have been discouraged, although some, such as Calvin, did recognize prophetic qualities in respected leaders of their movement. Even if the title 'prophet' was not often applied to those within the church of those days, much of the preaching of such outstanding figures of church history contained elements of prophetic insight which led to a new direction for many of God's people. In chapter 10 we must ask whether we can see signs of Christian prophecy in the church today.

For further thought and discussion

1. Why do you think Christian prophecy became scarce in the early church? (See 1 Thes. 5:19–22.)
2. Can spiritual gifts fall into disuse by default? What neglected gifts were renewed and widely encouraged at the time of the Reformation? Is the emphasis on prophecy today to be viewed in a similar way?

[1] Aune, *Prophecy in Early Christianity*, p. 338.

3. Why will all prophecy cease at the coming of Christ? What is essential to the nature of Christian prophecy which makes it valuable during these last days? Why will it become obsolete at the parousia?

10/Prophecy today?

The issues which we have been discussing are far from academic niceties. As we indicated in chapter 1, there is much confusion about prophecy in the church today, and we cannot ignore the matter in the hope that it will go away. There is every indication that prophecy will continue to be a controversial subject for some time.

Discernment

Of course, the New Testament encourages the church to be discerning. We must not only be able to distinguish between, on the one hand, the apostolic prophecy which was the true successor to the classical Old Testament prophetic tradition, and, on the other, the Christian prophecy which functioned in the New Testament church and, we believe, continues to be exercised. We must also be on our guard against *false* prophecy, and we must learn to distinguish what is good from what is indifferent among the insights which are sincerely offered by recognized Christian prophets.

For many evangelicals who are well versed in Scripture there is little danger of becoming sceptical about biblical authority or of being attracted to heretical cults. Theological liberalism and the teachings of the Moonies, for example, can be refuted by sound exegesis of Scripture. We can protect ourselves from such influence and defend and promote the historic Christian faith in a confident way (and in fact there is much evidence in the worldwide church that the conservative churches are growing while liberal churches are on the whole diminishing in size and influence).[1]

The real danger is from within. Within the evangelical fold we hear many voices which command our attention today. Parachurch activity is at a peak, with groups emerging which offer ministries to the whole church – there are specialists in healing, evangelism, prophecy, Bible teaching, and so on. Methods are being promoted as the solution to pastoral problems and systems are available for encouraging healthy growth for all disciples. While there is much worthwhile material on offer there is also much dross! But how are we to tell the difference between the helpful and the hurtful?

False prophecy

Jesus taught his disciples to watch out for false prophets (Mt. 7:15–23). He spoke of those who would try to infiltrate the church by posing as bona fide prophets when really wolves in sheep's clothing. Jesus warned his followers to be discerning. They should not accept everybody who claimed to bring a word of prophecy in the name of the Lord. They were to examine the fruit produced by such claimants: their character, and their influence on others. He went on to say:

[1]D. M. Kelley, *Why Conservative Churches are Growing* (New York: Harper and Row, 1972).

> Not everyone who says to me, 'Lord, Lord,'
> will enter the kingdom of heaven, but only he
> who does the will of my Father who is in
> heaven. Many will say to me on that day,
> 'Lord, Lord, did we not *prophesy* in your name,
> and in your name drive out demons and per-
> form many miracles?' Then I will tell them
> plainly, 'I never knew you. Away from me, you
> evildoers! (Mt. 7:21–23, *cf*. 24:23–24)

These stern words speak to a functional age. In
recent years we have been encouraged to believe
that the reality of God's presence in his church is
chiefly to be seen in mighty works. Congregations
are hushed as words of prophecy bring personal
messages from God to his people, often couched in
first-person language. Hundreds are moved as
people are apparently healed before their eyes in
large meetings. In pastoral work exorcisms are
carried out which claim to deal with problems that
have refused to respond to more normal remedies.
If the good news of what claims to be a new
movement of God's Spirit is to be passed on, those
who have witnessed such phenomena have to tell
others: 'If only you had been there! This man has
remarkable insights. This is what God is saying to
the church today. We must follow this pattern if we
are going to make an impact on a word-blind
world. This really works.'

In contrast to this Jesus said that even if 'it works'
there is a more important dimension. What are the
long-term effects on others? What aspects of the
character of Jesus are seen in those who engage in
such mighty works? As we have seen, Jesus spoke
plainly of those who claimed to prophesy in his

name but lacked the fruit of his Spirit in their lives and above all lacked a personal relationship with him. They were not known by Jesus. Because of that, what seemed to be good works were really the deeds of evildoers!

Let us assume, however, that we are determined not to be duped by such false prophets and that we can apply tests to prophetic claims and claimants. In our discussion so far we have noted that Paul, for example, had to warn the Thessalonians against being taken in by counterfeit prophecy which was supposed to have originated with him (2 Thes. 2:1–5). His advice was that they should compare such prophetic predictions with what Paul himself had said about the events surrounding Christ's return. 'Don't you remember what I told you?' was his rebuke. That advice covers a multitude of sins! In addition to the test of character and effect which Jesus taught, Paul emphasized the need for any purported prophecy to be in conformity with the word of God as already received.

John was also concerned to instruct his hearers about false prophets: 'Dear friends, do not believe every spirit, but test the spirits to see whether they are from God, because many false prophets have gone out into the world' (1 Jn. 4:1). He then went on to teach them how to recognize prophetic activity which was truly of the Spirit of God: 'Every spirit that acknowledges that Jesus Christ has come in the flesh is from God' (1 Jn. 4:2). This is the first test of whether believers should even listen to purported prophecy – do the prophets believe that Jesus is the incarnate Son of God? But John reminded his hearers (1 Jn. 2:20) that they had been anointed by the Holy Spirit and that they should allow the Spirit to guide them to apply to test prophetic claims in the light of the received apostolic truth.

The whole of 1 John provides guidelines for testing prophecy. False prophets have departed from the apostolic doctrine (1 Jn. 2:18–19). They have set themselves up as knowing better than the apostles (or of having the only true interpretation of what they have taught). Other pointers to look for are the morality of prophets – do they persist in blatant disobedience to God's law (1 Jn. 3:4–10)? And is there evidence in their lives of the sacrificial love of Christ (1 Jn. 3:11–24)?

1 John could be understood as providing timeless truths for the testing of what claims to be prophecy in the church. Nowhere does it suggest that Christian prophecy is obsolete. As the last survivor of the apostles, the aged John could have dealt with the matter simply by rejecting any prophecy which was not from the apostolic circle. That he did not do.

Our problem is that much of what is perceived as Christian prophecy would pass these tests. We may be impressed by the character and effectiveness of prophetic figures. We may not be able to find anything in their prophecies which contradicts Scripture. But is what they say truly Christian prophecy as described in the New Testament? Are we to take what they say and evaluate what God may be saying to his church through them? How can we learn to distinguish between elements which are to be received and those which should be rejected? How are we to act upon tested prophetic insights where that is the expected response?

To answer these questions, let us return to the seven scenarios (see pp. 14–17) of what purports to be prophecy in today's church.

Seven scenarios revisited

1. The house church movement

Andrew Walker's recent study of the 'Restorationist' churches in the UK explains the place of prophecy in the house churches.[1] The primary ministries of these fellowships, which Walker believes can be identified in terms of the teaching of Ephesians 4:11–16, are apostles and elders. Walker compares these to bishops and priests in the historic churches, and not without basis. While teaching on prophets, evangelists and teachers has been clarified in the movement, these ministries are not common in the house churches. Although there are many prophecies in their meetings, there are few formally (or informally) recognized prophets. In one branch of the movement, prophecies have to be submitted to the elders, who then decide whether to release the message for the whole congregation. In other places greater spontaneity is encouraged. Walker suggests that few local churches would claim to have one or more resident prophets. In fact, prophets are considered to be second only to the apostles of the movement.

The kind of prophecy described in chapter 1's first scenario is fairly innocuous. The young girl who is allowed to speak by the elders is sharing an encouragement which she feels God wants the

---

[1] A. Walker, *Restoring the Kingdom* (London: Hodder & Stoughton, [2]1988), pp. 147–153; see Appendix 2 (a), p. 205.

171

people to hear. But the terms are so general that one wonders if they could be described as prophetic in the New Testament sense. What she says does not seem to be predictive, or to give any insight into what God is doing in the world or the church, or to encourage deeper fellowship with the Lord. What makes it seem to be prophecy is that it is based on a vision, which she describes, and purports to tell God's people about his attitude toward them. The meaning of it could have been derived from general scriptural knowledge, and the phrases of her prophecy reflect the kind of things Old Testament prophets said when they were bringing words of comfort.

Such was my first-hand experience of that Bible-week meeting. My first impression of prophecy of that order was that it appeared to be claiming very little in terms of authority. It was certainly not perceived by me as a message which claimed to be the actual words of God to his people in any absolute sense. It may be that in such meetings prophecy is offered which is very low-key and certainly not offensive, like one experience I had when I was preaching during my student days. After the service one of the congregation thanked me for the sermon and said that he had a word for me based on a verse in Jeremiah. It was a word of encouragement which I have since forgotten! One wonders what effect it might have had if it had been a rebuke!

While much prophecy offered in the worship of 'Restorationist' churches may often be innocuous, Walker has recorded a prophecy which claims an authority of a different order. In 1974 one of the leaders of the movement gave a prophecy about the future ministry of a colleague:

> Say not that this is too high a calling. Think not that it is too large a sending. But I say to you that I who have purposed before you came forth of your mother's womb, will achieve in you that thing for which I have destined you ... And I will speak to you that you may speak to them. And they will know that God has spoken.[1]

It appears that this message, in the first person, was believed to be words from God. By this means a new apostle was chosen for the movement. Perhaps it was perceived as a parallel to the way Timothy was set apart by prophetic utterance (1 Tim. 4:14). It is unlikely, however, that Christian prophets would have spoken to Timothy in such a way in New Testament times. It is much more like the experience of Jeremiah's calling recorded in the Old Testament (Je. 1:4–8). It betrays the fact that in Restorationist churches prophecy may well claim a higher authority than might first appear to be the case. If any of the leaders of that movement believe themselves to be experiencing a restored gift of prophecy in the primary sense, proclaiming insights with a claim to absolute verbal authority, we would do well to reject their claims as spurious. Such prophecy, as we have shown, is unique to the foundational apostles of the church and has ceased since their demise.

There does, however, seem to be an awareness of the fallibility of Christian prophets within the

---

[1]*Ibid.*, p. 302.

Restorationist tradition. In the prophecy quoted from above, the following words are included: 'You have been conscious, too, of the weakness within yourself, conscious of your haste, conscious of your impatience, conscious of the times you've spoken when I did not speak.' This suggests that some prophetic words had been evaluated as not from God, despite the fact that they may have been couched in first-person language.

On the whole, Restorationists do not imagine that their prophecies have canonical authority. Yet the form in which they are presented has often given the opposite impression, and this should be a matter of great concern to those within that movement, and a matter that could easily be remedied.

In this scenario we see two tendencies which make us uneasy. If what claims to be prophecy seems to be fairly trivial, our readiness to evaluate its content will be limited. If prophetic claims appear to be couched in absolutely authoritative terms, as the first-person terminology tends to suggest, there seems to be no room for weighing what is said. The first extreme detracts from Paul's teaching on Christian prophecy; the second extreme adds a dimension which is simply not compatible with what Paul taught the Corinthians. In fact it seems dangerously near to the kind of situation which he was seeking to counteract in 1 Corinthians (cf. 1 Cor. 14:36–38).

2. Scottish biblical ministry

Readers outside Scotland may not be aware of a movement which has been growing since the end of the last war, largely within the national Church of Scotland. Our second scenario will be familiar to readers of the well-known evangelical theological journal *Evangel* in which an address delivered by a leader of that movement, William Still, has recently been published.[1]

A biographical sketch of William Still has been written by Sinclair B. Ferguson as an introduction to a collection of Still's pastoral letters.[2] Recently, on the occasion of his seventy-fifth birthday, a *Festschrift* was presented to him which included essays by Dr Ferguson and other leading evangelicals such as I. Howard Marshall, all of whom owe some debt to William Still's teaching ministry.[3]

Still has been minister of Gilcomston South Church, Aberdeen, since 1945. During that time he has established a congregation which prior to his arrival was threatened with dissolution. Through a commitment to the systematic exposition of the whole of Scripture, through preaching and Bible study, along with a deep concern for corporate prayer, William Still has, under God, influenced many people, some of whom are now serving within the ministry of the churches in the UK, and others who are missionaries overseas.

From time to time, through his pastoral letters which circulate widely, William Still shares his convictions about how to apply the principles to be gleaned from such a thoroughgoing study of Scripture. One such theme has been a deep concern that most churches are too complex in their

[1] W. Still, 'What of the Future?', *Evangel* 5/3 (1987), pp. 2–8.
[2] S. B. Ferguson (ed.), *Letters of William Still* (Edinburgh: Banner of Truth, 1984), pp. 7–18.
[3] N. M. de S. Cameron and S. B. Ferguson (eds), *Pulpit and People* (Edinburgh: Rutherford House, 1986).

structures. He has called for a simplification of church life, excluding all but the basic requirements for teaching, evangelism, fellowship and prayer. His congregation has no organizations or groups other than two Sunday services, a midweek Bible study and Saturday evening prayer meeting. Sunday School is for the under eights and older children are expected to sit with their parents in worship. I remember one evening service which I attended while a student. In those days Still might preach for over an hour, and the subject was the book of Job. Yet I was amazed to discover that the nine-year-old boy beside me was taking notes!

Children have also become a part of the corporate prayer life of the fellowship, and it has become common for younger children to participate. While many fellow ministers have not accepted that such changes were appropriate in their situation, Still has consistently offered insights which other church leaders have evaluated and acted upon or decided to reject.

The principal conviction which he has shared, however, that the church's greatest need is to be upbuilt through a systematic teaching of the whole word of God, has been widely applied. Through accepting that conviction as a prompting of the Holy Spirit, many other ministers have adopted an expository approach to preaching, the like of which may not have been exercised for quite some time (according to James Philip, whose ministry in Edinburgh has also been influential).[1]

[1] J. Philip, 'Expository Preaching: an historical survey', in Cameron and Ferguson (eds), *Pulpit and People*, pp. 5–16.

That William Still is seen as a prophetic figure in modern Scottish church history is clear. But is this kind of leadership an outworking of Christian prophecy?

In his recently published address William Still seeks to answer the question 'What of the future?' The subject-matter is provocatively prophetic in its survey of recent history in the light of biblical prophecy, especially focusing upon the place of the Jews within the purposes of God. Romans 9–11 is seen as indicating that Paul expected his own people, the Jews, to turn to Christ in large numbers as one of the eschatological signs of the imminent return of the risen Lord. Linking this with the Nazi Holocaust and the establishing of the state of Israel, Still asks whether in God's providence the conversion of the Jews will take place soon. He confesses that for some time he has had a hunch that we are on the edge of a very significant time, whatever happens. One possibility is that the turning of Jews to Christ will bring a new age of revival and growth for Christ's church throughout the world. Another is that we may be on the verge of persecution and a new dark age. A third possibility is that we are near to the parousia itself. As we are approaching the third millennium AD Still wonders whether this is itself significant. As Abraham lived two thousand years BC, so we live equidistant in time from the great divide of human history, the life, death and resurrection of Jesus. Does this indicate that God's purposes are approaching the consummation?

Here there is no hint of 'Thus says the LORD', or any claim to absolute verbal authority in what

177

is offered. Yet an overwhelming sense that we are on the verge of crucial times pervades everything he says. The purpose is to challenge Christian leaders and churches to get their priorities right:

> Oh, that a great insight from God would possess the ministry of the church in Scotland today, to cause every other purpose, however fine, and noble, and charitable, and gracious to pale into comparative insignificance until no other desire possesses preachers and people alike, but that the Word of God and prayer should dominate the church's life . . .[1]

This clarion call is accompanied by some guarded comments on what he considers to be the dangers of recent trends which, whether social-activist or charismatic in nature, as far as he is concerned militate against the centrality of God's word in the life of the church.

Is this Christian prophecy today? William Still's teaching ministry is the basis of his 'hunches' expressed in his address. But many a gifted expositor does not have the kind of prophetic conviction which we see here: a longing that the church would follow God's guidance and get back to God's priorities. This is surely the kind of thing that Aquinas understood to be the hallmark of prophecy in the church – not to offer new teaching on the nature and purposes of God but to give new direction to the church's life.

Paul's requirements seem to be met here. There are no claims to absolute verbal authority; insights are offered for evaluation; opportunity is given to

[1] W. Still, 'What of the Future?', p. 8.

those who hear and read to weigh what is being said. We can probably discern elements in the prophetic ministry of William Still which are common to other significant leaders in today's church who, like him, may well be relatively unknown outside their immediate sphere of influence.

3. 'Prophetic Word Ministries'

Our third scenario referred to a prophetic gathering organized under the auspices of Clifford Hill's journal *Prophecy Today*. In Jerusalem during Easter 1986, more than 150 prophets from all over the world attended a conference with a specific purpose – to determine what God was saying to the church at that time. Through prayer and Bible study a consensus was reached after much struggle, as Hill related in subsequent meetings. They believed that God was showing them through the study of Old Testament prophets like Haggai and Jeremiah that he was shaking the world through contemporary events and that Christians should not pray for the disturbance to stop but for it to take its course.

Clifford Hill is a gifted expositor of Scripture as well as an influential sociologist. These abilities are married successfully in his seminal book *The Day Comes*, which seeks to offer a prophetic view of the contemporary world.[1] In that work he begins by showing how the Old Testament prophets spoke to their comtemporary situation and he draws forth principles from Scripture which indicate how God deals with the nations in history. Like William Still, Clifford Hill believes that

[1]C. Hill, *The Day Comes* (London: Fontana, 1982).

179

there is considerable evidence that the closing years of this century will be significant. He too is convinced that God still speaks to his people through prophecy. But what does he mean by this?

Hill understands prophecy in the Old and New Testament to have one major purpose: to bring the word of God to bear upon the contemporary scene, chiefly through prophetic preaching. He also notes that in the early church there was a tendency to suppress prophecy, and suggests that this led to a neglect of the prophetic gift due to a fear of false prophecy. Despite the warnings of early church teachers such as Irenaeus, prophecy seems to have been neglected. Whatever may have been the expectation of the church in past days, Hill believes that we should expect God to speak to us today, as he promised to do in the New Testament. But what are we to listen for? And how are we to hear this prophetic word?

Hill suggests that we may discover what God is saying to us today through study of the Bible, prayer and an examination of empirical evidence (the facts of what is happening in the world today and in the churches in particular). According to Hill, prophecy is distinct from these three essential elements, but it may be confirmed by them. The task of the prophet is to help others to see what God is doing in the wider world and to relate the local situation to this overall picture. He is like a man with a newspaper in one hand and a Bible in the other, seeking to relate contemporary events to the flow of God's overall purposes.

Clifford Hill's concern is to understand the current international situation in the light of the word of God in Scripture and to see whether there is a specific word from God to our generation.

His analysis of modern history and sociology is very searching, and he draws many parallels from the Old Testament story. There is a clear call to Christians to dissociate themselves from the materialism which pervades modern culture, and to pray and work to influence the nations so that the hungry are fed and the arms race brought to a halt. God is calling the world to repentance, without which there will be a terrible disaster. There is a new need for urgency, and the church is too complacent. Before the world will believe the church must repent and seek a fresh anointing of the Spirit. Hill attacks the institutionalism, materialism, secularism, unbelief, division and spiritual impotence of the church in the Western world, applying scriptural principles to these perceived areas of weakness.

All this is admirable. But is it Christian prophecy? F. F. Bruce's comments in the foreword to the book are interesting. He notes that Hill bases his argument upon an interpretation of Isaiah 24–27, and agrees that there is indeed a contemporary relevance for this prophecy. Hill's book is a word from the Lord for today, but it appears to be the exposition and application of Scripture rather than Christian prophecy as we have come to understand that phenomenon. We might call it prophetic exposition or charismatic exegesis, because the connection of Isaiah's apocalypse with the world situation today is not something which arises purely out of exegetical study. The prophetic element, if it is present, is in the fact that

181

Dr Hill claims to have insight into how God's wrath is being revealed through the present world situation (*cf*. Rom. 1:18–32).

That seems to be consistent with Clifford Hill's self-awareness at the time of writing, in seeking to offer prophetic teaching which would enable Christians to hear what God was saying about the church and the world at that time. This is a dimension which every preacher must covet if he is to teach the word of God and relate the message in a living way to life as it is lived in the contemporary world. Many evangelicals have rightly reacted to the tendency among more liberal preachers to take Saturday's news headlines into the pulpit on Sunday so that preaching is perceived as socio-political comment rather than exposition of God's word. The danger of our conservative position, however, is to go to the other extreme and to teach the word of God in a vacuum, as if it were detached from real life. Preaching with a prophetic cutting-edge is desperately needed in today's church and world.

Since 1982, when Dr Hill published the above views, a change has clearly taken place in his thinking. His more recent writings, while developing some of the themes we have noted already, have a different emphasis.[1] Again he has sought to apply the message of Old Testament history and prophecy to today's world. But in his latest book Dr Hill claims to be passing on 'actual words that I heard from the Lord'.[2]

In July 1983 he had an experience which he

[1]C. Hill, *A Prophetic People* (London: Fontana, 1986); see Appendix 2 (b), p. 206.
[2]*Ibid.*, p. 143.

182

describes. A strong conviction, which he believed to be from God, came to him that those with prophetic insight from all over the world should be gathered to share what they felt God was saying in the contemporary situation. The result of this was the 1986 Jerusalem gathering. Dr Hill wrote down the words he believed God was giving to him.[1] The message is in the first person, as can be seen from the closing sentences: 'You must find prophets in every land and bring them together. I will show you the next step when they come together. I myself will be with you in this task.' The prophecy was tested and confirmed with a number of others who claim to exercise prophetic ministries, and they felt led to believe that God wanted them to convene a meeting in the Holy Land prior to Easter 1986. The Easter celebration would, they were assured, be a significant time.

I was privileged to attend one of the follow-up conferences after that gathering and had the opportunity to meet Dr Hill and his 'Prophetic Word Ministries' team. I was impressed by his grasp of the application of Old Testament prophecy to today's world and felt assured that what he said was of the utmost importance. I was also moved by the fact that during that conference it became clear that a particular problem was haunting many church leaders: the influence of Freemasonry in the Scottish church. I went home with a sense that God had confirmed what he was saying to our particular situation in specific ways. I was encouraged by that to share with other

[1] *Ibid.*

church leaders and pray over the matter further, with the result that an important part of what we sense to be on God's agenda for our time was brought out into the open.

In addition the overall conviction of their prophetic gathering, that God is shaking the nations and that we are on the edge of significant times, seems to be confirmed by much of what has been said by respected international Christian leaders including, as we have noted, William Still.

Yet there is one aspect which still leaves me hesitant. In Dr Hill's approach as reflected in his team's ministry there is now an emphasis on waiting on the Lord for specific prophetic words, often couched in the first person, which purport to be actual words from God. In fact Dr Hill in his latest book claims that, like Jeremiah, he has stood in the council of the Lord.[1] Because of that he has included in heavy type the words which he believes he has received from God. While they are quite scriptural in what they say, these prophetic statements claim to be 'on line' from God himself and could be misunderstood. I am not convinced that Dr Hill is claiming to speak with absolute verbal authority as Jeremiah did. But the danger of his presentation is that the valid insights he offers might be rejected by those who feel he is claiming too much for himself and his message.

We can see that Paul's distinction between apostolic prophecy which communicated the actual words of God and Christian prophecy which offered insights which were open to evaluation

[1] *Ibid.*, p. 151; *cf.* Jeremiah 23:18: 'But which of them [the false prophets] has stood in the council of the Lord to see or to hear his word?'

184

and testing must be maintained if today's prophets are to keep within biblical guidelines. It would be a tragedy if through imbalance valid and much needed insights were to be rejected as spurious.

Cecil Robeck, who was then teaching at Fuller Theological Seminary in California, commented in 1983 that he had become aware of a concern among leaders of the charismatic movement in the UK about this very issue. Within the movement were emerging a few leaders who were recognized at large as having prophetic ministries, but they were no longer willing to submit their prophecies to any form of testing. They argued that as their credentials as proven prophets had been established they had a personal authority which should be accepted when they spoke 'in the Spirit'.[1]

This is a very disturbing trend, and one I have also observed in more recent times. No matter how pointed may be the content of such prophecies, we are understandably distracted by the way in which they are presented and the authority which is assumed. It has even been suggested that such prophets have tended to promote sensationalism and have sometimes disseminated information about the state of the nation or world affairs without citing sources or corroborating evidence. In this latter respect Clifford Hill has set the standard in *The Day Comes*, in which he draws upon a vast array of data to substantiate his insights. It is my hope that any material which is circulated or published with a view to promoting

---

[1]C. Robeck, 'Prophetic authority in the Charismatic setting: the need to test', *Theological Renewal* 24 (1983), pp. 4–10.

prophetic ministries would be similarly backed up by evidence.

4. Radical evangelicalism

Jim Wallis, a noted American evangelical leader and social activist, has been acclaimed as a prophetic figure in recent years and has influenced the thinking of conservative Christians concerning social involvement. His establishing of a Christian community, the Sojourners, in a poor area of Washington, DC, has been seen as a significant step in recovering the whole gospel. The renewal of the church in recent years has involved a much-needed emphasis on getting alongside the poor and oppressed.[1]

We might compare such figures as Wallis with the Wilberforces and Shaftesburys of the past. They are Christians whom God has called to correct imbalances in Christian attitudes and lifestyle and to influence the governments of the world. We rightly think of them as being prophetic leaders who have under God changed the course of human affairs.

But although we may see a prophetic element similar to that discerned in the writings of Clifford Hill in the timely application of the particular parts of God's word needed to restore balance and effectiveness to God's church, we must ask whether Wallis is to be thought of as a Christian prophet in the Pauline sense.

As with Dr Hill, the danger might be to assume that because a Christian leader expounds the

---

[1]J. Wallis, *The Call to Conversion* (Tring: Lion Books,. 1982); *The New Radical* (Tring: Lion Books, 1983).

186

prophets of the Old Testament he is necessarily functioning as a Christian prophet. But it is not necessarily the case. He might be a gifted expositor, applying the message of the canonical prophets in a timely way. His ministry might in other words be as a teacher rather than a prophet. If he is applying ignored or forgotten principles which he has unearthed from Scripture, we suspect that he is acting primarily as a teacher of God's word, not as a prophet.

But if leaders like Wallis claim that God has shown them, for example, that there is a particular way to implement these lost principles, then we might do well to test their contributions as Paul encouraged. An example of this might be that having set up a Christian community in one place, believing that God wanted to establish a new kind of work in a poor area, such a leader wants to urge other Christians to do the same, feeling that this is a strategy which God has revealed to him which should be applied widely. Such prophetic packages have to be unpacked carefully and evaluated for the particular situations in which the churches worship and witness.

Discernment is required whenever a church leader says that the pattern of his own ministry is what the Holy Spirit is saying to the church at large. What has worked and been blessed in one situation may be a disaster in another! I cite this as an example of how, if we are rather loose in applying the prophetic accolade, the result might be the developing of a personality cult rather than a genuine expression of the fresh winds of the Spirit. Francis Schaeffer had a wonderful word for this which he seems to have invented:

187

stagnifying.[1] By this he meant taking an experience from the past which may have been valid and good in its original context and venerating it in the present in an entirely different context, with the result that the past experience becomes stagnant in the present.

This is not meant to be a criticism of Jim Wallis or his emphasis. I refer to this only in order to clarify what we understand as prophecy today. It is often not the fault of imaginative and pioneering leaders that their admirers sometimes make greater claims for them than they would make for themselves.

While Christian prophets in the New Testament church could have an itinerant ministry which extended across international boundaries and influenced different churches, the majority seem to have had a local ministry, and the insights they shared were largely for the local church. From time to time, however, patterns have emerged as a result of prophetic ministries which have reached far beyond the limits of local fellowships. John Wesley's 'method' of dividing his converts into class meetings is a good example. This is not something expressly taught in Scripture, yet there is evidence from the New Testament for Christians meeting in home groups. Wesley's prophetic insight for his day was that the time was right to establish a small-group structure once more. In recent years that emphasis has been recovered in many churches, but it would be unwise to suggest that such a pattern was necessary or that it always

[1] L. T. Dennis (ed.), *The Letters of Francis Schaeffer* (Eastbourne: Kingsway, 1986), p. 78. The word combines the verbs 'stagnate' and 'magnify' in a colourful way!

works (stagnification might result!). Some have gone so far as to say that it is not *methods* that God used but *people*. But true as that is the gift of prophecy in the church, where rightly used and discerned, does lead to the formulation of strategies and methods – yet without Spirit-filled people all such methods will fail.

5. 'Power Evangelism' and 'Power Healing'

I have already dealt at length with one phenomenon which has become controversial in recent years, the 'word of knowledge' which John Wimber has claimed is central to his healing ministry (pp. 97–109).[1] I suggested that the word of knowledge is in Pauline thought an aspect of the teaching of the whole word of God and not a phenomenon in which a believer is granted insights into the spiritual, mental or physical condition of another. Many people have said, however, that such 'words of knowledge' have indeed revealed amazingly accurate facts about their situation and that this has led to conversion or healing. What are we to make of this? Is it an aspect of Christian prophecy? Is it just that Wimber has confused the terminology and labelled a valid phenomenon wrongly?

Wayne Grudem has some interesting things to say about similar phenomena which are described in the writings of Jewish rabbis in sub-apostolic times.[2] One Rabbi Meir (AD 140–164) is recorded

---

[1] Donald Bridge has recently written at length, and helpfully, about Wimber's teaching. See D. Bridge, *Power Evangelism and the Word of God* (Eastbourne: Kingsway, 1987); see also Appendix 2 (c), p. 207.

[2] W. Grudem, *The Gift of Prophecy in 1 Corinthians* (Washington, DC: University Press of America, 1982), pp. 24–33.

as knowing as soon as he saw her, by means of the Holy Spirit, the substance of a quarrel which a woman had just had with her husband. Rabbi Gamaliel II (AD 80–120) had a similar experience when meeting a total stranger who was a Gentile. He immediately called him by his correct name, believing that the Spirit had placed it in his mind. Rabbi Hanina ben Dosa (AD 80–120) would pray over the sick and be able to predict whether they would recover. He also predicted, on his own death bed, the sudden death of another rabbi. Yet all these phenomena were not thought of as comparable with the authoritative predictions of the Old Testament prophets.

Grudem's concern is not to prove whether such things actually happened, but to show that it was quite possible to be faithful to rabbinic traditions and the belief that the classical voice of prophecy was no more to be heard, and yet to accept that such insights might be given by the Spirit. As Paul was brought up in such an environment under Rabbi Gamaliel I it is at least possible that he understood prophetic manifestations in the churches in a similar way, as promptings of the Spirit which were not absolutely authoritative in content yet which might contain elements of perception about the actual situations of people who were previously unknown to the prophet.

This has something to say about prophetic claims today. It shows us that during a time when prophets were operating in the early Christian church (see pp. 160–164), there were parallel claims in Judaism. This may have been one of the sources of the false prophecy which is warned against, for example, in 1 John. Such Jewish

prophets would certainly not have accepted that
Jesus was God incarnate! We may take two alternative routes in response to this. Either we say
that, *per se*, prophecy of this kind in Judaism was
always a counterfeit of demonic origin which was
intended to side-track Christians and harden Jews
in their resistance to the messianic claims of Jesus;
or we may accept that it is possible for genuine
'telepathy', or whatever we want to call it, to occur
in many different settings, Christian or otherwise,
so that it would be unwise to seek to corroborate
such phenomena purely by reference to, for
example, John 4:1–42 and 1 Corinthians 14:24–
25.

I leave the reader to apply the principles which
we have sought to draw out of the New Testament
and to test the claims of those who practise this
kind of thing as a regular part of their ministry. If
such insights must not be called 'words of knowledge', are they part and parcel of Christian prophecy? Is it not possible that a true prophet might
have a strong conviction about the personal situation of another, as Agabus clearly experienced
when he came to Paul to tell him about his
approaching imprisonment? Yes, it is possible;
but remember that Agabus was not accurate in his
details, and it is very unwise to imagine that such
purported insights are always correct.

In fact, so slender is the evidence for such occur-
rences in the New Testament that it would be
extremely unwise for any church leader to suggest that they should become central to the ministry of the church and be promoted as a method of
pastoral care. There is no hint in 1 Corinthians
that the function of Christian prophecy was to act

as a prelude to healing or counselling. In fact healing is not mentioned in 1 Corinthians 14:26–40 as a component part of worship at all. The normal context for healing in New Testament times seems to have been in visiting the sick (Jas. 5:14–16).[1] The danger of the widespread exercise of the 'word of knowledge', however we label that phenomenon, is that Christians will expect the extraordinary to become commonplace. They will hunger for subjective experience which is detached from the word of God, and prophetic utterance as a prelude to signs and wonders will become the focus of their interest, rather than the preaching of Christ crucified. That is bound to lead ultimately to disappointment and frustration, as deep human needs are not always as clearly definable as some would suggest. Pastoral problems are often quite complex and not easily solved. It is often part of the mysterious work of the Holy Spirit to apply the teaching of God's word to lives in a quiet and unspectacular way, as the message is prayed into the hearts of the people. Yet we cannot deny that the Spirit does from time to time choose more dramatic methods.

This trend towards focusing on prophetic phenomena is a reversal of Paul's teaching, where Christian prophecy is clearly referred to as secondary to the teaching of God's word and is subject to its authority. Our experience must be tested by Scripture, not vice versa. It is quite mistaken to take what may be genuine, yet extraordinary, modern phenomena and read them

[1] D. J. Tidball, *Skilful Shepherds* (Leicester: IVP, 1986), pp. 287–294.

back into the everyday experience of the New Testament church.

I offer this tentatively, from a pastor's perspective, concerned that those who are at present committed to the view I have sought to question might reconsider their position. I am sure that John Wimber and his colleagues are sincere Christians who have many gifts and insights. It may be that they have extraordinary abilities to understand the problems of others. In calling such insights 'words of knowledge', however, they have sought to make a regular working of the Spirit out of something which is not even specifically listed among the *charismata*. And even if this was modified and thought of as being part of the prophetic gift there is very little justification on the basis of the New Testament for the regular exercise of prophecy as a means of communicating detailed insights into the personal situations of others. When such insights are given they are quite extraordinary and are not depicted in the New Testament as part of the normal ministry of Christian prophets.

6. Personal prophecies

Early on in our present ministry we received a visit from friends who work as pastor and wife in a well-known congregation in the London area. We were just beginning to find our way around our new parish and were gaining understanding of the situation in the church. It was too early to have come to any conclusions about the real needs of the people or where they were spiritually.

Our friends spent a day with us and prayed with us that God would bless our ministry. A few days later we received a letter in which a message was included; a word of encouragement from the Lord. The message was written in the first person, as if God himself was addressing us and our situation. It encouraged us not to be fearful but to be bold in love and went on to speak about the real needs of the congregation and how we were to seek to meet them.

The message is too personal to include in print, but I share this to assure my readers that prophecy has not been a purely academic interest for me. I have found that the general thrust of this message has been borne out over the years. Had it come later on in our ministry one might have doubted its validity. But as neither our friends nor ourselves had any in-depth understanding of our situation at that time the accuracy of its insights is remarkable.

I confess that I am unhappy with the fact that the prophecy was communicated in the first person. I take this as a sign of the fallibility of Christian prophecy and not as a pointer to false prophecy. I would encourage others not to couch such insights in the first person but to offer them as humbly as possible, in the belief that the Holy Spirit has prompted the thoughts. Then they will be received, as Paul encouraged, as insights which need to be tested and evaluated.

I am convinced that personal prophecy like this is a valid expression of the secondary type of prophecy which we have discerned in the New Testament. It may be that it is particularly appropriate when new beginnings are being made. Remember that Timothy was set apart as an evangelist and preacher with prophetic utterance being made about his ministry (1 Tim. 1:18; 4:14). Perhaps those of us who are called to leadership in the church should especially seek the prophetic gift so that we might be instrumental in encouraging others for particular service.

It is interesting that, apart from the congregational context of Christian prophecy in the New Testament, the only other scenario presents prophecy as being offered to church leaders at crucial points in their lives. Do we not need such guidance and encouragement today?

7. Reformed reaction

The seventh scenario has already been dealt with at length in chapter 9. As I have already made an appeal in this chapter to my charismatic brethren, let me conclude with an appeal of a different kind to those who may have disagreed with much of what I have said. For many of my colleagues who share in the Reformed faith, the position I have adopted will seem to be at best questionable and at worst threatening. To many the words 'prophecy' and 'prophet' are so bound up with their commitment to the verbal inspiration of Scripture that to suggest possible alternative interpretations will seem to undermine the canonicity of the New Testament itself.

J.I. Packer, however, has helpfully responded to the claims of those who have suggested that Christian prophecy has died out completely, as well as to those who have imagined that it has only recently been restored.[1] He suggests that Christian prophecy is not a renewed phenomenon which should

[1] J. I. Packer, *Keep in Step with the Spirit* (Leicester: IVP, 1984), pp. 214–217.

be clothed with first-person terminology to distinguish it from other forms of Christian communication over the last eighteen or nineteen centuries. He says: 'We should realize that [prophecy] has actually been exhibited in every sermon or informal "message" that has had a heart-searching, "home-coming" application to its hearers, ever since the church began.'[1]

Packer asserts that prophecy is a reality wherever the message of the Bible is spelt out and applied, whether from the pulpit or more informally. If by 'application' Packer means more than the general application of principles, we would agree that such prophetic preaching or discussion is an important part of the exercise of Christian prophecy. We have already demonstrated, however, that prophecy should not be equated with an aspect of preaching. Preaching may include prophecy, but not all who prophesy are necessarily preachers (see pp. 82–86).

The important point to note is that, like Aquinas, Packer sees the prophetic dimension in the area of providing direction to the church's activities. To think of prophecy in all its forms as necessarily tied to the apostolic age is quite unnecessary. And if such an erudite Reformed scholar as Packer can feel secure with such a thought I am sure that many others can too!

Packer is also understanding towards his brethren who may have adopted the first-person phraseology of some charismatic prophecy, encouraging them to be weaned off this practice with its inherent pitfalls, while accepting that

[1]*Ibid.*, p. 217.

people have received encouragement even if the form of words could have been better!

Packer is unashamed to see a marked distinction between apostolic prophecy and prophecy which continues to be exercised in the church, although it is not clear from this particular book whether he would accept the two-fold division we have adopted.[1] While he may arrive at this conclusion by a different route we believe that it corroborates the basic thesis of the present argument in many ways. It is possible to accept that there is prophecy in the church today without trembling for the ark of Scripture!

Prophecy now

Our seven scenarios have introduced us to a controversial area of discussion which, increasingly, we shall not be able to avoid. My hope is that this book will encourage further study and, above all, understanding between evangelical Christians who may hold different views on the subject. Let those who make greater claims for their prophetic insights than is warranted by the New Testament beware of the danger of adding to God's word. Let those who deny the existence of Christian prophecy be careful lest they subtract from it.

If, as our survey in this chapter has suggested, there is widespread conviction that we are on the edge of very significant times for the church and the world, surely we must pray that preachers and

---

[1] Packer's comment on W. Grudem's *The Gift of Prophecy in the New Testament and today* (Eastbourne: Kingsway, 1988), which propounds such an interpretation, is, however, that it is 'careful, thorough, wise and to my mind convincing' (cover commendation).

people will be open to the powerful application of the word of God with prophetic insight and the prophetic contribution of lay people in prayer fellowships, discussion groups and leaders' meetings. Only then will we receive the guidance and direction that God wants to give to his church in crucial times. But if, in reaction to what we think are dangerous trends, we stifle the prophetic word, how can the body of Christ be built up?

For some pastors, acceptance of the fact that the church is called to be a prophetic people may produce one simple result: they will learn to listen as well as to teach, and not be afraid to establish opportunities for their congregations to pray and discuss the word of God in small groups. In addition, they will become more sensitive to the opinions of others who share with them in the leadership of the church. Perhaps they might even expect prophetic insights to be given at elders' meetings!

Whatever the outcome, prophecy will one day cease, at our Lord's return. It is not the most important aspect of church life, as Paul reminds us: 'For we know in part and we prophesy in part, but when perfection comes, the imperfect disappears ... And now these three remain: faith, hope and love. But the greatest of these is love' (1 Cor. 13:9–10, 13). We may be able to prophesy, but without love it is all pointless (1 Cor. 13:2). So, in our eagerness to prophesy or in our hesitation about the whole issue, let love be our chief concern, as Paul, our mentor, has said: 'Follow the way of love and eagerly desire spiritual gifts, especially the gift of prophecy' (1 Cor. 14:1).

198

For further thought and discussion

1. Discuss ways in which prophecy might be emphasized at the cost of love. What can we do to encourage both prophecy and love in the church?

Postscript: Prophecy in the 'last days'

As in chapter 10 we gathered our thoughts together with a call to Christian love, so our final word must be a challenge to Christian discernment. Jesus would not have sounded his warning in Matthew 7:21–23 were it unlikely that many of his followers would be susceptible to influence by false prophets. As we earlier noted, they are likely to come from within the evangelical fold: wolves in sheep's clothing (Mt. 7:15, 23) who have prophesied, exorcised and performed miracles in Jesus' name.

Paul warned the Thessalonians not to be easily unsettled by fake apostolic prophecy (2 Thes. 2:1–3) which contradicted scriptural teaching. A hallmark of the *last days*[1] – the period between the first and second comings of Christ – would be, according to Jesus' prophecy in Mark 13:22–23, the appearance of false claimants: 'For false Christs and false prophets will appear and perform signs and miracles to deceive the elect – if that were possible. So be on your guard; I have told you everything ahead of time.' Yet it seems

---

[1]See Acts 2:17; 1 Tim. 4:1–4; 2 Tim. 3:1–5; Heb. 1:1–2; 1 Pet. 1:20; 1 Jn. 2:18.

that Paul expected this deception to intensify as the parousia draws near:

> Don't let anyone deceive you in any way, for that day will not come until the rebellion occurs and the man of lawlessness is revealed, the man doomed to destruction ... The coming of the lawless one will be in accordance with the work of Satan displayed in all kinds of counterfeit miracles, signs and wonders, and in every sort of evil that deceives those who are perishing ... So, then, brothers, stand firm and hold to the teachings we passed on to you, whether by word of mouth or by letter.' (2 Thes. 2:3, 9–10, 15).

The warnings in Paul's 'famous last words' in 2 Timothy are even stronger: 'But mark this: There will be terrible times in the last days ... Evil men and impostors will go from bad to worse, deceiving and being deceived' (2 Tim. 3:1, 13).

Paul's antidote to such deception is clear. We can be protected from false prophecy only if our faith is thoroughly grounded on the balanced teaching of the whole Bible. One of the greatest dangers we as evangelical people face is to exchange our biblical inheritance for a mess of 'prophetic' pottage! Recent studies show how this has already begun to take place in the United States.[1] Are we aware of the fact that we too may be seduced away from the truth, the whole

---

[1]See D. Hunt and T. A. McMahon, *The Seduction of Christianity* (Eugene, Oregon: Harvest House, 1985), and the sequel *Beyond Seduction* (Eugene, Oregon: Harvest House, 1987).

truth and nothing but the truth? Let us not lose sight of our priorities:

> But as for you, continue in what you have learned and have become convinced of, because you know those from whom you learned it, and how from infancy you have known the holy scriptures, which are able to make you wise for salvation through faith in Christ Jesus. All Scripture is God-breathed and is useful for teaching, rebuking, correcting and training in righteousness, so that the man of God may be thoroughly equipped for every good work (2 Tim. 3:14–17).

It is under the supreme authority of Holy Scripture that Christian prophecy must be placed, as part of the training and equipment of God's people. But the instruction manual is, and must remain, the written word of God, with which we must test all claims to prophecy now, as then: 'Do not put out the Spirit's fire; do not treat prophecies with contempt. Test everything. Hold on to the good. Avoid every kind of evil' (1 Thes. 5:19–22).

For further thought and discussion

1. Do you think that we are on the edge of significant times? What should Christians do in reaction to such premonitions?

PROPHECY TODAY? Opinion poll

Please answer the following questions and return them to me. Please answer all the questions without further research, to indicate your present response. Please do not put your name on this form.

1. **Do you consider yourself to be a prophet or to have a prophetic ministry?**

   YES: 51% NO: 30% DON'T KNOW: 19%

2. **In the life of your congregation, where would you expect prophecy to be exercised?**

   (i) Through preaching: YES: 83% NO: 10% DON'T KNOW: 7%
   (ii) In elders' meetings: YES: 38% NO: 45% DON'T KNOW: 17%
   (iii) In house groups: YES: 42% NO: 42% DON'T KNOW: 16%
   (iv) In Bible study/prayer meetings: YES: 65% NO: 18% DON'T KNOW: 17%
   (v) In secular work of members: YES: 20% NO: 48% DON'T KNOW: 32%
   *(vi) Nowhere: YES: 12% NO: 88%

3. **By whom would you expect prophecy to be exercised?**

   (i) By ministers only: YES: 12% NO: 75% DON'T KNOW: 13%
   (ii) By men only: YES: 11% NO: 74% DON'T KNOW: 15%

4. **Is New Testament prophecy the same phenomenon as Old Testament prophecy?**

   YES: 37% NO: 43% DON'T KNOW: 20%

5. **Is prophecy a spiritual gift which God no longer gives to his church?**

   YES: 16% NO: 74% DON'T KNOW: 10%

6. Please indicate if you are aware of what the following have written about prophecy in recent years:

(i) Clifford Hill:	YES: 23%	NO: 77%
(ii) Jim Wallis:	YES: 31%	NO: 69%
(iii) John Wimber:	YES: 38%	NO: 62%
(iv) David Watson:	YES: 65%	NO: 35%
(v) Donald Macleod:	YES: 35%	NO: 65%
(vi) David Hill:	YES: 6%	NO: 94%
(vii) Wayne Grudem:	YES: 5%	NO: 95%

7. What office do you hold?

Minister: 90%   Elder: 4%   Others: 6%

(*In 2 (vi), a 'Yes' implies that the respondent did not expect prophecy to be exercised at all.)

Appendix Two:
Examples of prophecy today

(a) Prophecy in Restorationism

' The Sealing of George Tarleton', referred to by
Andrew Walker in *Restoring the Kingdom* (London:
Hodder & Stoughton, [2]1988), pp. 49–51, contains
details of a vision and a prophecy which was
claimed as confirming the calling of George Tarleton as an apostle in the house church movement
on 7 April 1974. Walker assembled from tapes of
the meeting the actual words spoken by Bryn
Jones, one of the leaders of the movement. Here
we include his prophecy:

> Say not that this is too high a calling. Think not
> that it is too large a sending. But I say to you
> that I who have purposed before you came
> forth of your mother's womb, will achieve in
> you that thing for which I have destined you.
> For you have heard this night from my ser-
> vant, of the calling of destiny. You have heard
> already of that hand heavy upon one. And you
> have known this in your own life.
>   But you have been conscious too of the

weakness within yourself, conscious of your haste, conscious of your impatience, conscious of the times you've spoken when I did not speak. But this does not disqualify you. For I being mindful of this will choose you and still send you. And I will make up all the cracks, and I will fill up all the gaps within you that you may fill the gaps in others.

And I will draw your scattered thoughts together, that you might draw together their scattered thinking. And I will speak to you that you might speak to them. And they will know that God has spoken.

You shall not stay in any one place beyond my time of appointment. But you shall go in, close the rank, and come back swiftly, says God.

George Tarleton remained an apostle in the Restorationist movement until 1984. Walker recorded this prophecy in his book with Tarleton's permission.

(b) Prophecy in the writings of Clifford Hill

In *A Prophetic People* (London: Fontana, 1986), p. 143, Dr Hill records in bold type actual words which he believes that he heard from the Lord in July 1983 concerning a future prophetic gathering in Jerusalem:

When you see this, your heart will rejoice and you will flourish like grass; the hand of the Lord will be made known to his servants, but his fury will be shown to his foes (Isaiah 66:14).

206

This day I am fulfilling my word. Today I am calling forth my servants the prophets from every land to come together and seek my face that they may proclaim my word to the nations. I have not left myself without a witness in this generation. I have spoken to my servants and they shall speak my words to the people.

Today you are to call them to come out from among the people and nations and seek me together, that my word may be known among them and heard among the nations.

Be strong and of good courage and you will see the unfolding of my will and you will go out with joy and will sing of the faithfulness of your God.

You must find my prophets in every land and bring them together. I will show you the next step when they come together. I myself will be with you in this task.

The prophetic gathering took place at Jerusalem and Mount Carmel over Easter 1986.

(c) The 'word of knowledge' in John Wimber's writings

In *Power Healing* (London: Hodder & Stoughton, 1986), pp. 252–273, he includes a report by Dr David A. Lewis, a social anthropologist, on 'words of knowledge', which were manifested at a Wimber conference at Sheffield in October 1985. The report is prefaced by the following examples of 'words of knowledge' which Lewis observed during plenary sessions at that time:

'There is a woman here whose name begins with L... She is thirty-two years old, has had a throat condition for eight years, and has taken medicine for it but it hasn't helped her.'

'There is a woman with a grumbling appendix, and I don't know if she knows it or not but she is pregnant too!'

'There is a young man here, about thirty-five years old, with a lot of problems in his marriage. He lives in the Midlands. He has been thinking this week about leaving his wife but the Lord wants you to stay and be reconciled with your problems. Do not leave your wife.'

About 2,800 persons were present at that conference.